Anonymous

The Roman Mass in the English Church

Illegal services described by eye-witnesses

Anonymous

The Roman Mass in the English Church
Illegal services described by eye-witnesses

ISBN/EAN: 9783743407152

Manufactured in Europe, USA, Canada, Australia, Japa

Cover: Foto ©Lupo / pixelio.de

Manufactured and distributed by brebook publishing software (www.brebook.com)

Anonymous

The Roman Mass in the English Church

THE

ROMAN MASS

IN THE

ENGLISH CHURCH

ILLEGAL SERVICES
DESCRIBED BY EYE-WITNESSES

First Series

Reprinted by permission from THE RECORD

WITH INTRODUCTION AND NOTES

SECOND EDITION

London
CHAS. J. THYNNE
WYCLIFFE HOUSE, 6, GREAT QUEEN STREET, LINCOLN'S INN, W.C.
1899

CONTENTS

	PAGE
ST. MICHAEL AND ALL ANGELS, NORTH KENSINGTON	1, 76
ST. CUTHBERT'S, PHILBEACH GARDENS	6
ST. ALBAN'S, HOLBORN	11
ST. MICHAEL'S, SHOREDITCH	14
ST. MATTHEW'S, WESTMINSTER	17
ST. MATTHIAS', EARL'S COURT	19
ST. AUGUSTINE'S, KILBURN	25
ST. SAVIOUR'S, POPLAR	29
ST. PETER'S, LONDON DOCKS	33
ST. ALPHEGE'S, SOUTHWARK	37
ST. STEPHEN'S, LEWISHAM	41
CHRIST CHURCH, CLAPHAM	45
ALL SAINTS', LAMBETH	50
ST. MARY MAGDALENE, BRADFORD	54
ST. JOHN THE EVANGELIST, UPPER NORWOOD	59
THE CHURCH OF THE HOLY REDEEMER, CLERKENWELL	63
ST. AGNES', KENNINGTON PARK	69
ST. ANSELM'S, STREATHAM	73
ST. AUGUSTINE'S, SETTLES STREET, STEPNEY	79
ST. CYPRIAN'S, MARYLEBONE	85
A "SUNG MASS" AT THE CHURCH OF ST. MARY AND ST. MARY MAGDALENE, BRIGHTON	87
THE TEACHING AT ST. ANSELM'S, STREATHAM	94
AT ST. PETER'S, VAUXHALL	98
SOLEMN EUCHARIST AT ST. AGATHA'S, PORTSMOUTH	103
CHILDREN'S EUCHARIST AT ST. MICHAEL'S, PORTSMOUTH	108
ANOTHER VISIT TO ST. ANSELM'S, STREATHAM	110
THE ROMAN MISSAL IN ENGLISH CHURCHES	113
THE ROMAN MISSAL IN ENGLISH CHURCHES. II.	123
THE EXTENT OF THE RITUALISTIC MOVEMENT	135
NOTES	138

INTRODUCTION

THE following pages are an attempt to show by the stubborn testimony of facts that the present condition of the Church of England demands the serious attention of all who value the work which was accomplished by the great Reforming Divines of the sixteenth century. That work has been steadily and stealthily undermined during the last fifty years, and every effort has been made to reimpose upon the people of England the corrupt and superstitious teaching of the Church of Rome. Much of the real meaning and ultimate purpose of this movement has been veiled under the specious and sophistical plea that the Church of England before the Reformation was independent of the Church of Rome, and that the Reformers, while rejecting certain papal aggressions and assumptions, wished to maintain the continuity of doctrine unimpaired. Ritualistic controversialists repudiate the charge of Romanism by laying stress upon their denial of the papal authority, and by magnifying trivial variations of "use" by which the pre-Reformation Church in England was distinguished from Rome. The unreality of this claim on behalf of doctrinal continuity is shown by the fact that those who assert it find the provisions of our present Prayer-book unequal to their requirements. They are compelled to obtain from other sources the ritual and order which will harmonise with the doctrines they teach. They do not scruple to restore practices which the Church to which they belong has condemned and rejected. They go further, and introduce from modern Roman sources practices of which the pre-Reformation Church had no knowledge. The reports of services in Ritualistic churches here given will afford some idea of the lengths to which the movement has gone. They are not the occasional eccentricities of a few extreme men. In every part of London, in every important provincial town, and in hundreds of villages throughout the country services similar to those described are regularly taking place.

These reports, which appeared first in the pages of the *Record* newspaper, have contributed materially to the formation of that public opinion which the Bishop of London said, in a letter to Mr. T. Cheney Garfit, the Bishops required in order to enable them to act. They are now reprinted, by the courteous permission of the editor, in response to the request of many readers, who wished to have them in a more permanent form. They originated in the following way. The Bishop of London, whose attention had been called to the Corpus Christi celebrations which were reported in the *Record* of June 10th, 1898, sent on June 14th the following memorandum to all the incumbents in his diocese:

"REV. AND DEAR SIR,—There are some points relating to the performance of Divine Service to which I think it is well to direct the attention of the clergy.

"In a diocese such as this, where there is so much work to be done of a missionary character, and where the circumstances of parishes vary so greatly, it is natural that there should be a tendency to make new experiments in various ways. This natural tendency has affected the conduct of public worship, and must, in some degree, always do so. But it is a tendency which must be subject to certain obvious limitations, to which I would call your attention. It is absolutely necessary that nothing should be done which affects the due performance of the services of the Church as laid down in the Book of Common Prayer, and that any additional services which are used should conform entirely to the spirit and intention of the Prayer-book. There must be no confusion in the minds of the people as to the standard of worship in the Church of England,

and there must be no opportunity for personal eccentricities to invade the system of the Church. No seeming advantage to the methods of teaching pursued by an individual teacher, as suited to a particular congregation, can compensate for the harm which is done to ecclesiastical order by any infringement of these principles.

"For the guidance of the clergy I think it well to give a few directions on points which I know to have caused some perplexity and dissatisfaction.

"(1) Morning and Evening Prayer should be said and the Holy Communion be celebrated on Sundays at such hours as are most convenient to the congregation. There should be no appearance of disregard of any one of these services in favour of another.

"(2) The service for Holy Communion should be said as it is appointed in the Book of Common Prayer, without additions or omissions. It should be said in an audible voice throughout.

"(3) Additional services, where used, should be separated by a distinct interval from the services appointed in the Prayer-book, and should be announced as additional.

"(4) These additional services are, I am aware, for the most part of a very simple kind, consisting of psalms, lessons, and prayers taken from the Prayer-book. They are adapted to special classes, such as services for children, or for men or women, or members of parochial guilds or organizations; or they are intercessions for special purposes, such as Missions, or temperance, and the like. I need not say I have no wish to restrict the use of the church for such purposes of devotion; but I think it right that in all cases such service should be submitted for my sanction.

"In making known to you my wishes in these matters I would express my deepest sympathy with the arduous work in which you are engaged, and with the difficulties which beset you in dealing with the many problems which it must needs raise in your minds. But it is my duty to see that permissible liberty be not unduly extended, so as to impair the distinctive characteristics of the services of our Church.

"Commending you and your labours to the blessing of God, I am your faithful servant in Christ Jesus,

"M. LONDON."

With prompt and somewhat surprising docility seventy-three incumbents, chiefly belonging to the more "advanced" section of the London clergy, sent the following reply to their Bishop:—

"LONDON, *June 30th*, 1898.

"MY LORD,—We desire to assure your Lordship of our dutiful and loyal compliance with the directions contained in your Lordship's circular, and at the same time having regard to the nature of those directions, to thank your Lordship for having vindicated the character of your clergy, as priests and gentlemen, from the aspersions cast upon them by some Members of Parliament."

It will be observed that the Bishop expressly states that the service for the Holy Communion should be said as it is appointed in the Book of Common Prayer, without additions or omissions. It should be said in an audible voice throughout. Now, in Ritualistic churches there are constant interpolations, having a definite doctrinal import, in the Communion Service. The chief of these are probably the singing of the *Benedictus qui venit*, or "Blessed is He that cometh in the name of the Lord," before the Prayer of Consecration; and the *Agnus Dei*, or "Behold the Lamb of God which taketh away the sin of the world," at its conclusion. The object of these additions is first to prepare the minds of the congregation for the supposed coming of Christ into the elements of bread and wine upon the altar, and then to lead them to worship their Lord "under the forms of bread and wine," as if then and there brought down from heaven by the words of the priest. This is not an exaggerated statement. It is but the obvious meaning of the addition of these two anthems, of the ringing of bells and the prostrations of body and the subsequent elevation, and "many such-like ceremonies," at this part of the service, and is no more than the admitted teaching of scores of Ritualistic manuals. But whether they have a meaning or not, the Bishop says there are to be *no additions* to the service for Holy Communion, and the seventy-three clergy promise "dutiful and loyal compliance" with this direction. They further thanked the Bishop for having vindicated their characters as priests *and gentlemen* from certain aspersions which had been cast upon them. Now if there is one characteristic which more than another is usually supposed to belong to a gentleman it is that of truthfulness. A gentleman is not bound to pledge his word, but, having once done so, he is bound to keep it.

Much curiosity was naturally felt as to the extent to which these gentlemen would modify their services in accordance with this profession of compliance with the directions of the Bishop, and special correspondents of the *Record* visited personally a number of the more prominent churches, whose incumbents had signed the letter. The results given speak for themselves. They show for one thing that some at least of these "priests and gentlemen," having voluntarily and publicly promised to obey the directions of their Diocesan, neglected to keep the promise thus made. There is no question here of the disputed interpretation of obscure rubrics. The lawfulness or otherwise of particular ceremonies does not enter into the matter. But on three points, viz., the audibility of the service throughout, the absence of additions, and the absence of omissions, a definite pledge was given. There were of course other points in the Bishop's circular which were similarly treated, as in the ostentatious disregard shown for the service of Morning Prayer as contrasted with the Holy Communion. The above three particulars have, however, been singled out from the others, as they raise a clear and distinct issue; and it may be said again that there was no need for these priests to have pledged themselves to obey certain directions, but if they wished to retain the title, of gentlemen there was need that they should have kept their word.

These reports are not, however, confined to the churches

whose incumbents signed the above letter, nor are they in fact restricted to the diocese of London. The object in multiplying them, even at the cost of some repetition of details, has been to show how widely-spread and deeply-rooted are the practices described. Their chief lesson is that in the case of the one service upon which more than any other the Reformation in England turned, the work of the Reformers is being undone. The Holy Communion is again being changed into the Roman Mass. The sacred rite which our blessed Lord instituted as a feast of which all were to partake is changed into a priestly performance which the congregation may witness, but in which they may take no part. This fundamental subversion of the teaching of the New Testament and the Prayer-book is of far greater moment than the introduction of services for blessing ashes or venerating crosses. It shows more than anything else can that, to use the concluding words of an able leading article upon the subject in the *Record*, "the English people are really confronted by a powerful, well-prepared, and energetically led crusade, the object of which is to supersede High Church and Low Church alike, and to make the Church of England the counterpart in teaching and worship of the Church of Rome without the Pope."

It is only necessary to add that the Editor of the *Record* is in no way responsible for the Introduction or the Notes which accompany these reprints.

THE ROMAN MASS
IN
THE ENGLISH CHURCH

───◆───

ST. MICHAEL AND ALL ANGELS, NORTH KENSINGTON.

Vicar: REV. PREBENDARY H. P. DENISON.
Patrons: THE TRUSTEES.

CORPUS CHRISTI SERVICES.

THE feast of Corpus Christi which is annually kept in a growing number of the more extreme churches, is, as is well known, a comparatively modern institution. It is not English, but distinctively Roman; there is no shadow of precedent or excuse for its use in the English Church. The brief account in Hook's *Church Dictionary* gives its history as follows:—

"A Roman festival instituted by Pope Urban IV., 1264, and observed on the Thursday of the week after Pentecost. The institution was the natural result of the acceptance of the doctrine of Transubstantiation. The festival was established in honour of the consecrated Host, and with a view to its adoration."

Perhaps, too, we may as well recall some of the circumstances which led to the foundation of the new festival. They began with a nun of Liège, who in 1230, whilst looking at the full moon, saw a gap in its orb, and "by a revelation from heaven" learned that this typified the want of a new feast, that of the adoration of the body of Christ in the consecrated Host. The "vision" of the nun was, a generation later, followed by a mysterious experience on the part of a monk. When going through the ceremony of Benediction he saw drops of blood fall on to his surplice, which presently formed themselves into images of the Host. This seems to have been decisive. Urban IV. soon afterwards ordained the new feast, promising absolution for from forty to one hundred days to the penitent who took part in it.

Such is the origin and character of the feast which the Confraternity of the Blessed Sacrament keeps year by year with great solemnity.

The parish magazine of St. Michael and All Angels, North Kensington, boldly marks in its Kalendar the "Eve of Corpus Christi" and the "Feast of Corpus Christi." For the "Eve" on Wednesday, the notice promised "Solemn Vespers of the Blessed Sacrament, Sermon and Procession, 8.30." It is difficult to understand how the services of the English Church can be accommodated to the needs of a Roman Corpus Christi celebration, or what relation "Solemn Vespers of the Blessed Sacrament" has to the Prayer-book which Prebendary Denison and his helpers have solemnly promised alone to use. The following account of the proceedings on Wednesday evening, from the pen of a careful correspondent, may be read with interest:—

"I reached the church in good time, and found it rather more than half filled; but there was a very small proportion of men, and the women, though they entered into the service with much interest, did not seem to be, as a whole, drawn from the educated classes. On the walls of the church were affixed some tawdry pictures intended to represent the Stations of the Cross, but only two of them were paintings with frames, and these two were each surmounted by a gilt cross. There was a side 'altar,' with a lamp burning before it, in the north transept. The 'High Altar,' which was crowded with candles, forty-seven in all, and had what appeared to be a 'Tabernacle,' had five lamps burning before it. There were two or three clergy in birettas and cassocks walking about the church, and arranging the members of the local guild of the Confraternity of the Blessed Sacrament. Most of the congregation were provided with the 'Manual' published by the Confraternity, and the service appeared to be taken from it; certainly it was not in the Prayer-book.

"At 8.30 the choir and clergy entered, led by two youths vested in scarlet cassocks, cottas, and scarlet caps, bearing two huge brass candlesticks holding lighted candles of proportionate size. Several of the choir were similarly attired, others had purple cassocks and cottas but no caps, while the cassocks of the remainder were black. Two of the clergy wore magnificent copes of richly embroidered silk and velvet. The service began by the singing of parts of Psalms cx., cxi., cxvi., cxxviii., and cxlvii. These Psalms were sung as a solo to Gregorian chants by one of the choir, who stood near the organist, some of the people joining in very quietly. Certain versicles not in the Prayer-book, such as 'May the children of the Church be as olive branches,' were introduced by the singer at the beginning of the Psalms.

"This over, the officiating clergyman, after genuflecting to the 'altar,' recited the passage, 'Brethren, I have received of the Lord that which also I delivered unto you,' &c., during which two acolytes lit the largest candles, ten in number, on the 'altar.' A hymn—309 in *Ancient and Modern*—was then sung, whilst the remainder of the candles on the 'altar' were lighted, together with fourteen candles which stood before a picture of the Virgin and Child on the north wall of the side chapel—the Lady Chapel, as it may perhaps be called.

"The *Magnificat* then followed, and during the singing of this a bewildering series of evolutions took place, members of the choir in twos and fours going up to the 'altar,' bowing, and then returning to their places at apparently irregular intervals, but with the precision of a regiment of soldiers on parade. At the same time two acolytes with censers approached the 'altar' together with the priest, and after the incense had been lighted several parts of the 'altar' were 'censed.' Then a tall youth 'censed' the choir, beginning on the north side and apparently 'censing' them in divisions according to the colour of their cassocks He bowed to each division as the ceremony was concluded, and then, coming to the chancel gate, 'censed' the congregation *en bloc*, bowing to them also and making the sign of the cross with his head as he bowed. The bowings were returned in each case, and then the priest and a number of those with the scarlet cassocks proceeded to the side chapel and 'censed' the 'altar' there also.

"After this followed the sermon by the Vicar, who took two texts, 'He that increaseth knowledge increaseth sorrow' (Eccles. i. 18), and 'As sorrowful, yet alway rejoicing.' (2 Cor. vi. 10.) It was an earnest, but not very pointed sermon, chiefly remarkable for the constant assertion of 'the Real Presence in the Blessed Sacrament,' and the ignoring of the question that it was not the fact, but the nature of the 'Presence' which divided Churchmen. He said that the members of the Confraternity of the Blessed Sacrament had the great gift of discerning the Presence, which gift had, in the mysterious providence of God, been

St. Michael and All Angels, Kensington

denied to so many of their fellow-Churchmen. They were like the young man in Dothan, whose eyes were opened to see the armies of heaven. The armies were there all the time, and so is the Presence, though those who discern it are in a minority in the branch of the Church to which they belong.

"At the beginning of the sermon the candles were all extinguished, but the relighting of them was a sign that the discourse approached its conclusion. There was an offertory for the 'Sanctuary Fund,' from which the expenses of this elaborate ritual are defrayed. This having been taken, preparations were then made for what was obviously the chief feature of this service, viz., the procession.

"Headed by a tall acolyte swinging his censer, the choir and clergy slowly moved from the chancel, and proceeded at a carefully measured pace round the church. A great number carried lighted candles, some carried banners, and others processional crosses; the two clergy in copes were respectively near the beginning and the end of the procession; a second youth swinging a censer brought up the rear. A large number of the congregation, doubtless members of the Guild, but chiefly women, joined in the procession, which, after going twice round the church, proceeded slowly up the central aisle towards the 'altar,' the members of the congregation quietly resuming their places.

"What does the Bishop of London think of these Corpus Christi ceremonies?"

ST. CUTHBERT'S, PHILBEACH GARDENS.

Vicar: REV. H. WESTALL.
Patrons: THE TRUSTEES.

I REACHED the now notorious church of St. Cuthbert's, Philbeach Gardens, Kensington, where Mr. Kensit made his protest against the service for the Veneration of the Cross, shortly after eleven o'clock on Sunday morning. There was a fairly large congregation assembled there, and Matins was in progress. The Vicar was conducting the service, and I should like to add that his tone and manner were both devotional and impressive. Although there was another service—"Choral Eucharist" —due at 11.30, there was no undue hurry, and except for the interpolation of a psalm or hymn between the second lesson and the *Benedictus*, one could follow it with one's Prayer-book without difficulty. Matins was ended shortly after 11.30, and choir and clergy left the chancel, and some of the congregation left the church. The greater number, however, remained—and they were reinforced by new-comers—to be present at the Choral Eucharist. There were six tall candles alight on the "high altar," which with its handsome crucifix, vases of flowers, and altar card enclosed in a highly-polished frame presented a striking appearance; and shortly before the beginning of the 11.30 service two young men in scarlet cassocks and cottas came into the chancel from the vestry, and, after making a bow in front of the altar, proceeded to light the two standard candles, one on either side of the altar. This done, the procession of choir and clergy, headed by the cross-bearer, entered the chancel. The choir had been considerably augmented since Matins, and the rear of this part of the procession was brought up by the Vicar and a curate, each of whom was simply attired in cassock and surplice. But the procession of the celebrant was much more gorgeous. He was preceded by a number of stalwart young men vested in scarlet cassocks and cottas, while he himself wore a green-coloured chasuble, that being the colour, I believe, according to the Roman use, and a biretta. All made obeisance towards the altar, the celebrant ostentatiously taking off his biretta and bowing towards it two or three times before he took up his position in front of it.

I do not propose to give a fully detailed account of the service, for the simple reason that I had only my Prayer-book with me, and there were so many things interpolated that I cannot say quite what they were. I see that the *Daily News* of Monday says that "the service was not of a very extreme character," but whether your readers will be of the same opinion after they have read what follows I very much doubt.

When the celebrant had prepared the censer a psalm —I think the forty-third—was sung, during which the celebrant, the altar, and the choir were censed. Then the celebrant, standing in front of the altar at the south end, began the Communion Office as we have it in the Prayer-book. All went well, except that the celebrant read very quickly and in exceptionally low voice, until the Epistle, which was read by the Vicar, who left his stall in the choir and proceeded to the south side of the altar for the purpose.

The reading of the Gospel was not, however, so simply accomplished. The Gospel-book was reverently moved by one of the numerous servers or acolytes in attendance upon the priest from the south side to the north side. The priest himself remained for some moments bowing in the middle of the altar, and apparently engaged in private devotions. When he approached the Gospel-book he was again censed, as was also the book. Then after saying "The Lord be with you," and the people answering "And with thy spirit," he announced the Gospel, and read it, facing north-east. Finally he kissed the book, and returned to the middle of the altar. The Nicene Creed was sung to an elaborate setting, the celebrant, choir, and people standing meanwhile.

The sermon followed. It was preached by the Vicar, who before giving out his text announced as days to be observed in the week St. Swithin *and St. Osmund*. Amongst other notices he asked for prayer for several dead persons whom he named. The sermon was based on the text, "Launch out into the deep," taken from the Gospel for the day. It was not particularly remarkable except for two very distinct references to current controversies. He spoke of the Apostles as strong, stalwart men—men who understood what muscular Christianity meant—and he went on to add that it might yet be necessary in the Church to do as Nehemiah did, work with one hand and carry a weapon in the other. There was also another lesson from the command, "Launch out into the deep," which was particularly applicable to them to-day. As a Church they had too long been influenced by insular prejudice and national use. They talked of the Church *of* England when they ought rather to speak of the Catholic Church *in* England. What was wanted was that they should launch out into the deep of God's Holy Catholic Church. Let them hold closely to the faith of their fathers, and they should see mighty results. The reference was somewhat cryptic, and the preacher left his meaning to be inferred rather than suggested it. At the close of the sermon Mr. Westall took off his stole, kissed it, laid it over the pulpit, and returned to the choir, and the service proceeded.

There were numerous little details preparatory to and following upon the placing of the elements upon the altar, which were quite new to me, but it was not until the Comfortable Words were reached that anything startling took place. Then, even while the priest was reading them, two acolytes proceeded to light the candles, which stood in two candelabra—seven in each—upon the altar. Four of the other young men attending on the priest left the sanctuary for the vestry, but they returned in a few moments, each one carrying in his hand a great standard candle lighted. They knelt in front of the altar on a step below the priest, and the scene was of a most brilliant description. The altar was a blaze of light. The Sursum Corda, the Preface, and the Sanctus were sung, the celebrant, servers, and people prostrating themselves at the words "Holy, Holy, Holy." The *Benedictus*—" Blessed is He that cometh in the name of the Lord; Hosanna in the Highest"—was interpolated before the Prayer of Humble Access. I presume that the Prayer of Consecration was said next. *But it was absolutely inaudible*, yet I was sitting in the fifth row from the chancel. The ritual, however, left no one in doubt as to what was taking place. When, as I suppose, the priest reached the words "This is My Body," a bell in the chancel and the bell of the church were rung three times, the young men held their candles aloft, and the priest immediately held up high above his head a wafer, whereupon the people bowed as low as they could. This was repeated, only with the cup instead of the wafer, at—here, again, I can only conjecture, for the priest was not audible—the words "This is My Blood." The priest himself continually genuflected during the Prayer of Consecration in a manner which suggested the worship or adoration of the elements. The *Agnus Dei* was then sung, and the priest seemed to be engaged in some private devotions of his own. He certainly bowed himself to the altar a great many times, and appeared to be continually making the sign of the cross over the elements; but seeing that he remained with his back to the people all the time, it is not possible to speak with any certainty. The young men with the candles afterwards left their position in front of the altar and moved to the side, and the celebrant turned half round and held up a wafer, whereupon the people again prostrated themselves. But the movement of the celebrant and his attendants was only momentary, and if it was intended to give anybody who desired it the opportunity of communicating it was futile for the purpose. As a matter of fact *no one communicated.* The vessels were ceremonially cleansed, and after the *Gloria in Excelsis* the *Nunc Dimittis* was sung, the priest and his attendants grouping themselves in front of the altar.

I leave others to point the moral of this service in the light of Mr. Westall's declaration of his "dutiful and loyal compliance" with the directions of the Bishop of London that "the service for Holy Communion should be said as it is appointed in the Book of Common Prayer, without additions or omissions. It should be said, in an audible voice throughout."

ST. ALBAN'S, HOLBORN.

Vicar: REV. R. A. J. SUCKLING.
Patrons: DEAN AND CHAPTER OF ST. PAUL'S CATHEDRAL.

AS one of the best-known of "advanced" churches in London, St. Alban's, Holborn, naturally suggested itself to anyone who wished to see how the signatories to the recent "Submission of the Clergy" interpreted their subscription to that brief and interesting document. I went at half-past ten, at which hour the ordinary service for Morning Prayer is held. The north side of the church, which is reserved for women, seemed quite full from end to end; the opposite side, where the men sit, had scarcely a score of persons in it as the service commenced. At exactly half-past ten a solitary priest, vested in cassock and surplice and wearing neither hood nor stole, entered the chancel and went through the Order for Morning Prayer at an almost incredible speed, though it was not at all difficult to hear what was being said. There was no music of any kind, the Psalms, Canticles, and even the *Te Deum* being read verse by verse alternately by the minister and people. In order not to lose time the minister recited the *Gloria* as he was proceeding from the prayer-desk to the lectern, and began the *Te Deum* and *Benedictus* respectively as he returned. I have never been at a service which seemed to me more irreverently and unintelligently performed. My experience was so precisely that recorded by Lady Wimborne in the *Times* that I should have thought her ladyship had visited the same church, had the hour of service and the number of clergy not been different. From beginning to end the Morning Prayer, without, so far as I remember, any omission, occupied only twenty or twenty-two minutes. During the whole of the service there was a constant noise caused by people entering the church, and when it was over I found that about three-fourths of the space allotted to men was filled up, and by eleven o'clock the church seemed, except for a number of seats on the south side, completely full. Then the chief service of the day began; the organ pealed, and clergy, acolytes, and choir entered. There were scarlet cassocks, gorgeous vestments, lighted candles, and all the other accessories of elaborate and advanced ritual. I saw "three men in green," the sight which greeted Dean Stanley's astonished eyes when he visited St. Alban's many years ago; and before what I suppose must be called High Mass began these three clergy marched from the chancel to the west end of the church and back, while the choir sang " Purge me with hyssop, and I shall be clean ; wash me, and I shall be whiter than snow." I could not see the aspersion of holy water, which ceremony is performed at this time; nor did any of the water reach me, as I was too far from the middle aisle. The Mass was then proceeded with. There were the usual censings, bowings, genuflections, lighting of candles, the bewildering crossing and recrossing from side to side of the chancel and up and down the steps of the altar. The Commandments were quite inaudible or rather unintelligible. The Gospel was read at the north wall of the chancel, the priest facing the wall, surrounded on three sides by acolytes with lighted candles, while a thurifer from time to time swung his censer. At the Creed the servers in red cassocks and most, or all, of the congregation sat down. I was unable to discover the reason, but I noticed that the rubric orders the contrary. The Prayer of Consecration was less audible even than the Commandments, and during several parts of it I could not discover that the celebrant was speaking at all. At several points while it was being recited the Sanctus bell rang. The bell in the church tower was also rung. There was no opportunity for anyone to communicate, and certainly no one made any attempt to do so. A chant, the words of which I could not distinguish, and the *Agnus Dei* immediately followed the Consecration Prayer.

One thing which struck me about the service was the dulness of it. There was a great deal going on in the chancel, which was interesting at first, but soon became somewhat wearisome; and the congregation was practically silent, having apparently no part to take in the service beyond watching the clergy and choir. The smell of incense, at first not unpleasant, made the atmosphere heavy and oppressive as the service proceeded.

The Sacrament was, I think, "reserved" in the chapel at the west end of the church. So far as I could judge, no alteration, either in the church or its services, has resulted from the "godly admonition" of Dr. Creighton.

ST. MICHAEL'S, SHOREDITCH.

Vicar: Rev. H. M. M. Evans.
Patrons: The Trustees.

IN the evening I went to St. Michael's, Shoreditch, the Vicar of which also signed the letter of submission. The church would be vastly improved if it were cleaned now and then, the dingy and dirty condition of the building being its most noticeable feature on a first inspection. The "Stations of the Cross" were hung round the walls, a side-chapel, which I presume was the Lady Chapel, having a sanctuary-lamp burning in honour of the reserved Sacrament. Many of the congregation as they came in went up to this chapel, and, going down on one knee, bowed reverently before taking their seats. A clergyman who passed across the church bowed right down before the side-altar, making only a slight inclination of the head as he passed the high altar. Outside the chancel screen were two figures—one of the Saviour, the other doubtless of St. Michael. Each was very highly coloured with scarlet and blue and gold, and each had a candle burning before it. On a nail on one of the pillars supporting the roof was a board with the following notice: "Asperges, page 2; Mass, page 51." I could not see any book in the church to which the notice referred, and the hymns at pages 2 and 51 of the Hymn-book afforded no clue to its meaning.

The opening exhortation in the evening service was

omitted, and the prayers were hurried through at a great rate. During the singing of the Psalms both choir and people remained seated, the choir rising at the "Gloria," the people merely bowing their heads. After the first lesson a hymn was sung, then the choir sang the words, "Master, we have toiled all the night and have taken nothing; nevertheless at Thy word I will let down the net." The *Magnificat* was then sung, and while this was being done a good deal of lighting of candles and incense burning took place. At its conclusion the choir again sang, "Master, we have toiled all the night and taken nothing; nevertheless at Thy word I will let down the net." Ignorance, I presume, is the cause of my inability to discover the reason for this apparently meaningless interpolation. Nor was it at all clear why the prayers for the Queen, the Royal Family, and the clergy were omitted.

Before the sermon, which was preached, I am told, by "Father" Black, a clergyman in a cassock and biretta gave notice from the pulpit that Mass would be said at the usual hours during the ensuing week, and urged the people to make a point of attending the weekday Mass. We were then asked to sing a hymn "to the praise and glory of God, and in honour of the precious blood of Jesus."

The preacher then ascended the pulpit, and having kissed his stole, delivered a sermon, which may be syllogistically summarised: "True religion is always persecuted. We are persecuted. Therefore we have the true religion." It was too much to expect that the underlying fallacy of the undistributed middle should have been generally recognised. The preacher having again kissed the stole, the sermon concluded.

One of the clergy attached to the church again entered the pulpit, and gave out a hymn, saying, "As we sing this hymn let us offer ourselves anew to our blessed Lord in the presence of His Holy Sacrament." Another hymn was then given out "as an act of reparation to our Lord for dishonour done to Him in His blessed Sacrament," and we were again urged to resolve, as we sang it, to attend weekday Mass more regularly. The hymn having been sung, the minister said, "Hail Mary," the congregation continuing, "full of grace, the Lord is with thee; blessed art thou among women, and blessed is the fruit of thy womb, Jesus. *Holy Mary, Mother of God, pray for us sinners now, and at the hour of our death. Amen.*" The minister then said, "May the souls of the faithful departed rest in peace." This concluded the service, there being no Benediction, and left me to wonder what the Vicar meant when he signed the letter promising obedience to the monitions of his Bishop.

ST. MATTHEW'S, WESTMINSTER.

Vicar: REV. W. B. TREVELYAN.
Patron: THE RECTOR OF ST. JOHN THE EVANGELIST, WESTMINSTER.

THE Vicar of St. Matthew's, Westminster, did not sign the letter of submission to the Bishop's authority, though it is believed that he would have done so but for the fact that he was too ill at the time for it to be shown to him. The church is situated in Great Peter's Street, quite close to the Great Smith Street entrance of the Church House, and it would seem to demand the early attention of the authorities. There is a massive wood screen with life-size figures of our Lord on the Cross, and of the Virgin and St. John on either side, and this is approached by a stone staircase. It is reported that there is a chapel at the top of the stairs where the Blessed Sacrament is reserved. There is also a side-chapel with altar, in addition, of course, to what I suppose I must call the "high altar"; but even these are not sufficient to supply the needs of the church, for on Sunday morning there was yet another altar—a temporary one—set up against the gate of the chancel screen for the purpose of celebrating the Children's Eucharist. The congregation consisted almost entirely of children, and the service was marked by ritual of an advanced character. There were several candles alight on the altar, the celebrant wore a red-coloured chasuble—this colour, I am told, denotes the Sarum use—incense was used, the *Benedictus* was sung, the Host was elevated and the children bowed down before it, bells were rung, the *Agnus Dei* was sung, and there were no communicants. After the Prayer of Consecration a young clergyman who was directing the devotions of the children from the back of the church called upon the children to make their act of worship, directing them to page 17 of some book they held in their hands. I have not succeeded in obtaining a copy of this book, so cannot give the exact words, but they were a distinct and definite statement of adoration of the body of Christ present in the Sacrament upon the altar. Later in the service the children were called upon to make their act of offering, and in doing so to pray for the Universities' Mission. Here, again, I cannot give the exact words used, but they referred to the offering up by the hands of the priests of the sacrifice of the Body and Blood of Christ. In neither case do the words form any part of the Book of Common Prayer. As I left the church I noticed a number of memorial cards in the porch—such as are to be seen at Roman Catholic chapels—begging you of your charity to pray for the repose of the soul of So-and-so.

ST. MATTHIAS', EARL'S COURT.

Vicar: REV. J. P. F. DAVIDSON.
Patron: THE LORD BISHOP OF LONDON.

THE following account of a visit to St. Matthias', Earl's Court, is interesting in view of the fact that the Vicar, the Rev. J. P. F. Davidson, was one of the signatories of the letter of submission to the directions contained in the Bishop of London's letter :—

There was a large congregation—mostly of fashionably-dressed people—at the service at St. Matthias', Earl's. Court, on Sunday morning. The interior of the church is calculated to impress a stranger, and there is a refinement and a "finish" about the appointments and decorations of the building which are not always noticeable in churches distinguished for their "advanced" services. The east end is specially remarkable. There are seven red lamps hanging before the altar, and these are kept, I believe, perpetually burning. The decoration of the altar is effectively arranged, with handsome gilt cross, candles, and an abundance of flowers, a beautiful design in colours and gold forming the background. On either side of the altar there are standard candelabra, but these were not used on Sunday. The chancel is shut off by an iron screen and gates. On the north side of the chancel there is a side-chapel with a second altar elaborately decorated, and here, I believe, the Sacrament is reserved. In any case, ladies of the congregation made obeisance towards this side-altar when taking and leaving their seats, and a small lamp surmounted the candelabra; but I am unable to say whether or no it was alight.

Matins was held at 10.30. The service was marked by reverence and devotion. There was no hurry; everything was done in order. It was, in fact, an ordinary congregational service led by a large and well-trained choir. There were no candles burning, but two gaseliers were lighted, and showed up the chancel well; otherwise it would have been somewhat dark. The senior clergyman present (presumably the Vicar) wore cassock, surplice, and biretta, which last he reverently took off when he had to pass before the altar, and at other times (*e.g.*, when he read the lessons) during the service. After the third Collect the Vicar made several announcements, amongst them being that certain daily services and the Children's Eucharist on Sunday morning would be discontinued until further notice. No reason was assigned for this. It was probably due to the near approach of the holiday season. He also stated that the Guild of the Confraternity of the Blessed Sacrament would say its office in the church one evening in the week.

The sermon followed. The Vicar ascended the pulpit, against the wall of which there is a crucifix, put on a green stole, having first kissed it, and announced as his text, "Oh pray for the peace of Jerusalem; they shall prosper that love thee." The sermon gathered up the lessons of the Dedication Festival, and in this connection the preacher expressed his disappointment at the small attendance at the week evening service, while the number of communicants on weekdays had been rather fewer than usual. He went on to plead for the new schools, and made a vigorous attack upon the School Board for its undenominationalism in religion. Finally, he spoke of present troubles. The text showed them in what spirit they must meet the agitation—

St. Matthias', Earl's Court

the spirit of prayer. There was no reason for alarm. The Church *in* England (though once he used the preposition "of") had passed through grave troubles before. Not so many years ago she had had to encounter the opposition of the Privy Council and the Prime Minister, and had emerged victorious over them all. If they acted in the spirit of the text they would find that prayer would give them faith. It was the littleness of their faith which made them afraid, and it was perfectly childish, said the Vicar with great emphasis, to talk of joining another Communion because of the agitation. Prayer would also give them tender consideration for their opponents. "Love your enemies" was their Lord's command. They could not expect to escape persecution, seeing that their Master was persecuted. Finally, prayer would teach them that God was in the midst of them. They sometimes talked as though they were the managers of the Church; but it was God's Church, and they had to remember the promise, "Thou wilt keep him in perfect peace whose mind is stayed on Thee." Truly they could say of the Church, "God is in the midst of her; therefore shall she not be moved."

The sermon ended, the offertory was collected, and the service was brought to a close with the Prayer of St. Chrysostom and the Grace, the State Prayers being omitted.

A large part of the congregation remained for the Choral Eucharist at 11.45, and others came in, but I was struck by the marked absence of men. Shortly before the beginning of the service two acolytes came in and extinguished the gas in the chancel, and lighted the six candles on the high altar. In a few minutes the organ pealed forth and the choir came in, passing through the chancel gates to the chancel, each boy and man bowing towards the altar as he passed to his seat. The celebrant's procession entered the sanctuary direct from the vestry without passing through the choir. The celebrant wore a green chasuble and a biretta, and was attended by eight or nine acolytes or servers, six of whom wore cassocks of bright red, cottas, and red skull-caps. There were the usual bowings as they approached the altar, and biretta and caps were taken off. The service began with an anthem (or is it called the Introit?), in which I could clearly distinguish the words "I will go unto the altar of God." It was beautifully sung, and the music was effective. It seemed to me, I may remark parenthetically, that whatever they do at St. Matthias' is well done from their own point of view ; there is nothing tawdry or commonplace about it. The anthem over, the celebrant began the Communion Office, standing in front of the altar at the north end. He was a young man with a good voice, and the service was audible throughout, although it was noticeable that at the Prayer of Consecration he lowered his voice. He read the Epistle from the south side, facing east. Following the Epistle came another anthem (or is it called the Gradual?), and then the priest crossed to the north side and read the Gospel facing north-east, kissing the Gospel Book at the close. The Nicene Creed, to an elaborate setting, followed. The celebrant was conducted to a seat on the south side of the altar after the opening sentences had been sung, but the choir and congregation remained standing. After the Creed the Vicar from his stall repeated some of the notices he had given out previously, and added a few more, amongst them being that Father (*sic*) Dolling desired to return thanks for a safe voyage, and he ended up with a request for prayer for certain dead persons.

Then began the preparations for what is evidently regarded as the chief part of the service. During the collection of the offertory the celebrant prepared the censer, and afterwards censed the various articles on the altar. Then, handing the censer to an acolyte, he stood with his

St. Matthias', Earl's Court

back to the altar while the young man censed him. This over, two acolytes came down the chancel and censed the Vicar, the choir, and finally the congregation. But the incense was used sparingly. The censing was carried out with considerable formality, the acolytes bowing towards each person or set of persons before they began, and their bow was returned at the close. Moreover, after censing one set they returned to the altar, and bowed to it before they approached another set. After the prayer for the Church Militant the service proceeded regularly until the Comfortable Words. Then, just before the *Sursum Corda*, four of the acolytes, who had gone to the vestry, returned to the sanctuary, each carrying a large lighted candle. They knelt two and two on either side in front of the altar, just below the celebrant, and at the *Ter Sanctus* they held their candles aloft. The *Benedictus* was here interpolated before the Prayer of Humble Access. More incense was used, and the Prayer of Consecration followed. At the words "This is My Body" the bell in the church tower was rung three times, and the priest elevated a wafer, whereupon the congregation bowed the head and worshipped. The priest, before proceeding with the consecration of the chalice, bowed himself before the altar in an attitude of adoration. The bell was again rung three times at the words "This is My Blood," the chalice was elevated, the people bowed, and the priest adored. The *Agnus Dei* was then sung. From this time onward until the close of the service the priest was constantly bowing down before the elements, and it would only weary the reader to describe it. There were no communicants, and, as far as I could see, no opportunity was given to anyone who desired to communicate. The priest certainly once turned to the congregation, holding the chalice in his left hand, and just above it in his right a wafer, as though he were about to drop it into the cup.

The movement was only momentary: he turned again to the altar and proceeded with the ablutions, and the service shortly afterwards concluded. After the Blessing an anthem was added, the words of which I could not catch.

I came away feeling that I had been present at what was the service of the Mass in everything but name. Your readers are probably better able than I am to say whether such a service is in accordance with what the Bishop of London calls "the standard of worship in the Church of England."

ST. AUGUSTINE'S, KILBURN.

Vicar: REV. R. C. KIRKPATRICK.
Patrons: THE TRUSTEES.

AMONG the group of better-known churches in London where "advanced" ritual prevails, St. Augustine's, Kilburn, holds a prominent position. It serves as a cathedral for the notorious Kilburn Sisterhood: it has been built and decorated at an enormous cost, and it has a large staff of able and energetic clergy. The Vicar was among the signatories to the letter promising submission to the Bishop of London's monition.

I went to the church on Sunday morning at 10.30, the hour for Morning Prayer. There was a large congregation, and the service was conducted according to the Prayer-book order, except that the sermon was introduced after the Third Collect, and the Prayers for the Queen, Royal Family, and Clergy were omitted. It was exceedingly difficult to join in the Gregorian chants which were used, and the greater part of the congregation made no effort to do so, though they joined very heartily in singing the hymns.

The sermon was based upon the first lesson, which recorded the numbering of the people by David, and the punishment which followed upon that act. The difficult question in the parallel passage, where God is said to have tempted David, was very carefully discussed. The pride of

David which led to his numbering of Israel was applied by the preacher to the "present distress." They (the "advanced" party) had thought with complacency and satisfaction of the work that had been done. They had pointed to churches not a few in which God might in some sense be said to be worthily worshipped, and the Sacraments not niggardly dispensed, and they thought that England was converted. But they had recently had a rude awakening, and had suddenly discovered that heresy was still rife around them. They had heard the language of the sixteenth century and not of the nineteenth. The shock was good for them—it served to disturb their pride, the last enemy which had to be destroyed in their spiritual life.

The references to heresy, which were obviously intended to apply to fellow-Churchmen who did not sympathise with the "Catholic" revival, did not impress me as an indication of spiritual humility, and your readers will probably not altogether share the regret expressed at the language of the sixteenth century being again heard. The preacher kissed his stole both before and after the sermon.

Morning Prayer being concluded, the clergy and choir left the chancel, and an interval of about ten minutes elapsed. A few people went out and a few more came in, but practically the bulk of the congregation remained. I was able in the interval to notice the church, which is a very handsome building, though, of course, designed in every part to represent the mediæval idea of worship. The chancel is rectangular, not apsidal, the Vicar having insisted upon this shape, as it is more English, the other being Continental. This is a fair illustration of the trifling variations in form, colour, or "use," upon which those who describe themselves as Anglican Catholics lay stress in order to show that they are not Romish. And this insular insistence upon trifling and almost frivolous variations in detail, where the primary and essential idea is the same, forms a great part of their controversial stock-in-trade.

There were seven sanctuary lamps burning before the "high altar," which by no stretch of imagination could be called a table; and a solitary lamp burning in the "Lady Chapel" indicated that the Sacrament was reserved. A massive stone screen, surmounted by six stone figures, divided the chancel from the nave, and effectually separated the clergy and choir from the congregation. On the wall of the church near the door was a long list of names headed by the inscription, "On whose souls, sweet Jesus, have mercy."

At 11.45 the choir and some clergy came through the church into the chancel, three other clergy vested for Mass, wearing green chasubles, and accompanied by acolytes, two of whom bore lighted candles, and another a huge processional cross, coming directly into the chancel through a doorway at the north wall, by which door they left at the conclusion of the service.

The antiphon, "We will go unto the altar of God," &c., was sung, and the Communion Service was proceeded with, the two standard candles and six on the altar having been lighted prior to the service. During the service two other candles on the altar were lighted. There were the same innumerable crossings from side to side of the chancel, and changing of the relative positions of the clergy, now in single file at the south side facing east, now three abreast, and then in single file at the middle, every variation of position possible to three men being apparently taken in turn. The altar, its ornaments, the clergy, the choir, and the congregation were duly censed. The Gospel was read by one clergyman facing due north, while another made a temporary reading-desk of himself, resting the upper part of the book on his forehead and holding the lower in his hand, while a cluster of acolytes with lighted candles and one with a censer stood round them, the whole presenting a remarkable and almost grotesque appearance. The whole congregation knelt down at the part of the Creed, "and was incarnate by the Holy Ghost of the Virgin Mary, and was made Man." They then rose and remained standing until it was concluded. The chant used made it difficult to join in repeating the Creed.

The *Benedictus qui venit* was sung before the Prayer of Consecration, and at the end of the Prayer there was a very long pause, much longer than I have noticed at any other church. The *Agnus Dei* followed. The Prayer itself was read distinctly throughout, a sacring bell being rung twice in the middle, in addition to the ringing of the bell in the church tower. After the singing of the *Agnus* the celebrant turned round and held up what appeared to be a large wafer, whereupon some members of the congregation, about twenty or twenty-five, went up to communicate, the great bulk of those present, who nearly filled the church, remaining in their seats. The service then proceeded, the ceremony of the ablutions being performed at its close. Although the words of the Prayer-book were practically adhered to, the Romanist "Ministers and Mistakers" of Edward the Sixth's first Prayer-book could not have more effectually disguised the character of the service.

ST. SAVIOUR'S, POPLAR.

Vicar: REV. R. R. DOLLING.
Patron: THE RECTOR OF POPLAR.

THE new Vicar of St. Saviour's, Poplar, was instituted by the Bishop of Stepney on July 22nd, 1898, and, having regard to the circumstances under which he resigned his charge at Portsea, it seemed to be a matter of some interest to ascertain in what way he would inaugurate his ministry at St. Saviour's. I accordingly proceeded to Poplar the following Sunday and attended Matins and the Choral Eucharist.

The parish is a poor one, and there are 10,000 people within its confines. The church is situated in a grimy-looking back street, where the houses are small and the inhabitants are many. It was nearly half-past ten, but the immediate neighbourhood did not seem to be half awake. I was not, however, quite prepared for what I saw in the church. The school-children and their teachers were there in force, but there was no adult congregation such as one looks for—even though it may be small at the East End—at Morning Service. The arrangement of the east end of the church suggested that the people were accustomed to a "high" service, but it was simplicity itself compared with the elaborate decoration of the "high altar" at some of the West End churches. On the retable there were two candles, a brass cross, and flowers; on either side of the Holy Table there was a banner, and a processional cross stood in the chancel. There is also a side-chapel, with Holy Table, and it is obviously used for service, but there was no evidence of Reservation. The new Vicar was present in his stall, but the service—simple, hearty, and reverent throughout—was conducted by one of the curates, Mr. Dolling reading the lessons. After the third Collect one naturally expected that there would be an address, such as would appeal to the juvenile congregation; but the Vicar explained to them that it was his first Sunday there, and it was his duty to read at that service something he was afraid they would not understand; but he hoped they would be as quiet as possible. And then, without further ado, Mr. Dolling, standing in his stall, read straight through the Thirty-nine Articles! It must have been an infliction to the young people, but they bore it patiently, and it was only when the Vicar was nearing the end that they became fidgety. During the service, and noticeably about eleven o'clock, a dozen, or perhaps twenty, people came in, and they remained for the Choral Eucharist. The children, however, went out at the close of Morning Prayer.

During the short interval between the two services the Vicar remained in his stall, wearing cassock and surplice. The adult congregation considerably increased in numbers, but the church was very far from full, and the number of men in the congregation was noticeably few. A server lighted the candles on the Holy Table, the organ pealed forth a voluntary, and shortly after 11.30 the choir entered the church from the west end. A number of the boys wore violet, but the men wore black, cassocks. The two curates brought up the rear of the procession, the one going to his stall in the choir and the other going within the sanctuary, accompanied by a server. The celebrant wore a long surplice, and as he approached the Holy Table both he and his server bowed towards it. The service began with a hymn, and closed with a hymn and the *Nunc Dimittis*. The *Agnus Dei* was sung after the Prayer of Consecration, and a hymn was sung during the communion of the people; but with these exceptions there was no variation from the order in the Book of Common Prayer—even the two long Exhortations were read *in extenso*—and the service was read in an audible voice throughout.

There were, however, one or two distinctive features to which attention may well be drawn. The celebrant began the service at the south side of the Holy Table, facing eastwards, and he also read the Epistle in the same position, the people kneeling meanwhile. The Gospel was read from the north side, the reader facing north-east. The Creed was sung to an elaborate setting, and the clergy went down on their knees at the *Et Incarnatus est*, and crossed themselves at the final words, "The life of the world to come."

The sermon by the Vicar followed. Mr. Dolling bowed as he passed in front of the Holy Table on his way to the pulpit, and, after kneeling in private prayer for a moment or two, rose, and, without preface of any kind, announced his text from the Gospel for the day, St. Mark viii. 1, "In those days the multitude being very great, and having nothing to eat, Jesus called His disciples unto Him." A very simple discourse followed. Mr. Dolling said he should be appalled at the great task before him, of seeking to minister to the needs of the ten thousand people gathered in the closely packed streets of that parish, were it not for the fact that he felt he was sent by One Who had compassion. He asked, with some feeling, for the prayers of the congregation that he might be strengthened for his work. They had, no doubt, heard many things about him. "Don't believe any of them," he said with a smile, "but just pray for me that as I minister to these people I may be filled with the compassion which filled the heart of our Blessed Lord."

After the Prayer for the Church Militant the celebrant gave notice of the next service of Holy Communion, and read at length the Exhortation for that purpose. This was followed by the Exhortation appointed for the time of celebration, and this he also read at length. The celebrant recited the Prayer of Consecration in an audible voice, but his genuflections before the elements immediately after the words, "This is My Body, which is given for you," and again after the consecration of the cup, together with the elevation of paten and chalice, conveyed an impression which was unmistakable in the minds of the congregation. And this impression must have been deepened when they saw the curate, who after the Prayer of Consecration left his stall for the sanctuary to assist in the communion of the people, genuflect before the chalice as it was handed to him, and the celebrant genuflect in the same way when it was safely in the assistant's hands. The long interval between the Prayer of Consecration and the priest communicating himself was also noticeable. There were about a dozen communicants, and the clergy, when administering the elements, made the sign of the cross with the bread and with the chalice in front of each person. The ablutions took some little time to perform, and finally the *Nunc Dimittis* was sung, the choir and clergy passing to the vestry at the west end of the church meanwhile. "Father" Dolling did not communicate nor take any public part in the service. Except when in the pulpit, he occupied his stall throughout.

ST. PETER'S, LONDON DOCKS.

Vicar: REV. L. S. WAINWRIGHT.
Patrons: THE TRUSTEES.

THE Church of St. Peter, Wapping, better known as St. Peter's, London Docks, ranks with St. Alban's, Holborn, among the earliest of the ultra-ritualistic churches in London. Everybody has heard of them both; but while St. Alban's attracts many visitors who merely wish to see for themselves what an "advanced" service is like, curiosity has tempted but few to stray so far east as Gravel Lane, Wapping. The district is certainly not inviting, and probably St. Peter's was on this account chosen by the brethren of the Confraternity of the Blessed Sacrament as the church most suitable for the holding of their annual private Synod. It is a fairly large and open church, with accommodation for about six hundred people; but from the outside it is at first a little difficult to gather the nature of the building. The notice-board is neither conspicuous nor ornamental, and might easily escape the attention which it well deserves, for it indicates the hour at which the "Litany of the Blessed Sacrament" is sung, the days on which confessions are heard, and other services, the names of which are not in the Book of Common Prayer. The church is approached through a somewhat forbidding archway under the Clergy-house, but I ventured across the courtyard and into the building. Almost the first thing to attract attention is a huge decorated cross, upwards of twelve feet in height, supported upon a beam at the base of the chancel arch, and filling the space between it and the apex. A substantial crucifix hung on one of the brick columns near the pulpit, which, as in all very ritualistic churches, is a comparatively insignificant structure. The Stations of the Cross are placed round the walls. There are quite a number of oil paintings representing different aspects of our Lord's Passion, the Virgin and Child, and similar subjects, while there are also several tawdry coloured prints like those to be seen in some Roman Catholic churches. Some banners, each surmounted by a gilt cross, leaned against the walls of the church, and a framed list of names near the porch appeared to invite prayers on behalf of the faithful departed, though I could not get near enough to read the inscription. Morning Prayer begins at 10.15 a.m., shortly before which time I arrived. There was no one in the church, except a few choir-boys on their way to the vestry, and until the service was more than half over I was the only member of the congregation; but towards the close a few persons who remained near the door came in. The service was clearly and audibly conducted according to the Prayer-book, except that the Prayers for the Queen, Royal Family, and Clergy were omitted.

At the close there was a brief interval, during which six of the candles on the "altar" were lighted, and while this was being done a number of strongly-built, powerful-looking gentlemen, whose somewhat *négligé* attire suggested that they resided in the immediate neighbourhood, filed into the church from a side, and apparently private, door. The greater part were arranged by one of their number, who appeared to be the leader, in the front rows of benches, while others were disposed in different parts of the church; an obvious and, in view of recent occurrences, perhaps not unnatural measure of defence. Including these auxiliaries the church was perhaps rather more than half filled by 11 o'clock, when the choir (which had been considerably augmented), the acolytes, and the clergy entered the chancel for the Communion Service. This did not differ materially from some of the services which have already been described in these pages. Incense was freely used, and lighted candles and processional crosses were carried about by the acolytes at various parts of the service. A sacring bell was rung before and twice during the Prayer of Consecration, the bell in the church tower being also called into requisition. During the service the remainder of the candles, making fourteen in all, upon the Holy Table were lighted. The acolytes, who at some churches are vested in scarlet cassocks and at others in black, wore what I believe are albs, drawn in at the waist with a cord or girdle. It would be tedious to describe the complicated and ever-changing positions of the clergy, or the crossings, bowings, and genuflections of the clergy and congregation alike; it would certainly not be easy to imagine anything more different from the general spirit of the Prayer-book. The *Benedictus qui venit* was introduced prior to the Consecration Prayer, and the *Agnus Dei* followed it. The prayer itself was in parts almost inaudible, and there were some long pauses in the middle and at the end. There was no opportunity given for the congregation to communicate, and the appearance of the gentlemen in the front rows augured ill for the result if anyone had made the attempt.

The congregation were asked to pray for the repose of the soul of some person who had died recently, and a very long pause which was made in the middle of the Prayer for the Church Militant seemed designed to afford an opportunity of doing so.

The sermon was a redeeming feature of the service. It

was preached from the text, "Not every one that saith unto Me, Lord, Lord, shall enter into the kingdom of heaven; but he that doeth the will of My Father which is in heaven." Having referred to the many sins by which those who either professed, or were believed, to be Christians were beset, the preacher singled out the vice of gambling, and gave a brief, practical, and helpful sermon upon the subject.

The ceremony of the ablutions was performed at the close of the service, after which the *Nunc Dimittis* was sung as the people left the church.

ST. ALPHEGE'S, SOUTHWARK.

Vicar: REV. A. M. CALCUTT.
Patrons: THE TRUSTEES.

LANCASTER STREET, Borough Road, is not the most attractive of thoroughfares, nor is St. Alphege's Church one of the most inviting, to judge by its exterior. The notice-board is, however, filled with announcements of services and lists of the various guilds, classes, and meetings in connection with the church. It states that the church is open for private prayer between two and five in the afternoon, but though I was there one day between those hours the building was securely closed. There is also a notice to the effect that on Sunday Matins will take place at 9.30 a.m. This statement is, however, considerably modified by a footnote, which says, "Subject to the staff of clergy." The footnote, however, reassures the reader by stating that there will always be a service at 11.30. This, of course, is the Communion Service, or, as the clergy there prefer to call it, "Holy Mass."

On Sunday morning last I went at 9.30, but the church was still closed, and there was no service then. I do not know whether Morning Prayer was said that day, but it possibly was, for though the *Tourist's Church Guide* agrees with the notice-board as to the hour of service, I found afterwards that the *Parish Chronicle* for July announced Matins on Sunday for 8.30, a somewhat unusual hour. The *Parish Chronicle* also announces that "the Vicar will usually be in church for confessions—Fridays at 11, 3, and after Evensong; Saturdays 3 p.m., and 6.30 to 9 (or later)"; and it moreover refers to the Holy Communion as "Mass," or "Sung Mass."

I returned at 11.30, at which time "Sung Mass" is announced, and found a large congregation—chiefly, however, made up of children, a very small number of adults being present. There was a notice on the wall by the door, saying that "no one will be allowed to communicate at the late Mass without notice being given *and permission obtained from the Vicar.*" The church is a fairly large one, but the brick walls, not being very clean, give it a gloomy appearance. In these are a series of coloured bas-reliefs with heavy frames, each surmounted by a cross, representing the Stations of the Cross, and there are a number of pictures, including a large one of the Crucifixion. The chancel is raised about three feet above the floor of the church, and, being very wide and open, gives some relief when the gas is lighted to the effect produced by the walls of the building. The "altar," which is raised several steps above the chancel, is a very elaborate structure, decorated with carving, and richly coloured and gilt. The ends projected considerably from the wall, forming a recess, and it did not appear that the edge of the altar came out beyond them—at least not sufficiently to allow of the north-end position being taken, even should the celebrant desire it. A number of candles were upon the altar, their chief characteristic being their remarkable height, and the chancel contained two standard candles, also of unusual height for the size of the building. There was a "Lady Chapel" and also another small chapel, but I could not discover whether the Sacrament was "reserved" in the former. I gather, however, that "reservation" will be practised, if it is not now, as the magazine states that the Lady Chapel is being put in order, and urges, "Let us with one accord put forth all our efforts, so that the chapel may be worthy of the Holy Mysteries

St. Alphege's, Southwark

which it is intended to contain." Seven large sanctuary lamps hung across the chancel, and there were banners and a processional cross against the wall.

Punctually at half-past eleven the clergy, choir, and acolytes —the latter in scarlet cassocks and cottas, and bearing processional cross, lighted candles, and censer—entered the chancel, and, after the singing of a hymn, the "Mass" proceeded. The tall candles on the altar, six in number, were lighted; but the standard candles were not, as the acolyte, after vainly trying to light one of them, gave up the attempt.

It would be hopeless, as well as fruitless, to attempt to describe the service in detail, the genuflections, crossings censings, and changes of position being innumerable. The Prayer of Consecration was to me absolutely inaudible, the ringing of the sacring bell and of the church bell being the only intimation by which I could learn what was taking place. There were no communicants, and no opportunity was afforded to any who might wish to partake, the notice near the door, quoted above, probably acting as a deterrent. The *Agnus Dei* followed the Prayer of Consecration, which was preceded by a hymn instead of the *Benedictus qui venit.* At the conclusion of the service the following two verses of thanksgiving were sung :—

> Great God, we thank Thee for Thy grace
> Of *hearing Holy Mass* this day ;
> On Sundays may we always come
> To hear the Holy Mass and pray.
>
> Then may the grace of Holy Mass
> Be with us still in all our need,
> And keep us from the state of sin
> In every thought, and word, and deed.

The clergy, choir, and people seemed to vie with one another in bowing to the altar, the persons who directed the congregation to their seats bowing each time. Contrary to my experience in many "advanced" churches, I received much polite attention from the church servants and those near me. More than once elsewhere I have been allowed to go through the whole service without even the offer of a hymn-book. This courtesy, however, does not appear to characterise the Parish Magazine, for after saying that "it is the greatest mercy that the new Vicar of Whitstable is a Catholic," it proceeds to reflect on his predecessor, a very excellent man, by the way, by saying that when away from St. Alphege (on a holiday, of course) "we may not feel *that we are in a heathen land.*" The magazine speaks of the clergy as "Father" Thelwall, "the Rev. Father Hydes," &c.; it informs us that it is hoped to revive the ward of the Confraternity of the Blessed Sacrament, which was given up when the "Order of Reparation"—whatever that may be— was established. The Feast of Corpus Christi, of course, was celebrated, "High Mass" being sung at 6 a.m., besides other Masses later in the day. The following paragraph from the July magazine—the only one I was able to obtain— well deserves the attention of the reader. The imposition of life vows, with the sanction of the Bishop of Rochester, seems far too serious a matter to be passed over in silence.

"On Saturday, June 25th, Sister Winifred was, *with the permission of the Lord Bishop of the diocese, professed for life,* to the honour and glory of God *and in obedience to the Order of Reparation of the Blessed Sacrament.* She has been a novice for $2\frac{3}{4}$ years, and proved by her devotion and zeal for the work of God in this parish her fitness to be professed, and her love for the poor and energy for their souls shows that desire which is so necessary for the true vocation of a Sister. At the same time two novices were received, Sister Hilda Mary and Sister Dorothea Mary, and we earnestly trust that they may prove worthy of their vocation and grow in grace, so that at the end of their novitiate *they may be accepted by Christ as His brides.*"

ST. STEPHEN'S, LEWISHAM.

Vicar: REV. CANON BRAMELD.
Patrons: KEBLE COLLEGE, OXFORD.

ONE of the impressions obtained from a series of visits to the ritualistic churches in and around London is that of the apparent want of uniformity in the conduct of the services. There seems to be no general rule to which they conform. The colour, shape, and size of the vestments, the number of candles, and a great many other details vary in nearly every case, and the variations do not appear to be affected by the financial condition of the neighbourhood, for in some very poor districts a more costly ritual prevails than in others where considerations of expense would hardly appear to enter. In many of these, however, it must be admitted that the cleanliness and general repair of the church fabric are sacrificed to the maintenance of its ritual. The one point, however, which marks them all is that they change the celebration of the Eucharist to such a degree that the other services appear of but little consequence in comparison, and that they entirely alter the character of the Eucharist from being a Communion by turning it into the Mass.

At St. Stephen's, Lewisham, some eccentricities found both in the east and west of London were happily absent when I went, but in all essentials the services were quite as "advanced." The church is a large, roomy structure, capable of seating about eight hundred persons, but an air of coldness and isolation, partly caused by the darkness of the building except during bright sunshine, appeared to pervade it. The heavy stained-glass windows seemed designed to allow as little light as possible to penetrate. A huge crucifix stands by the pulpit, and there are seven sanctuary lamps hung across the chancel, a large brass cross, six candles, and some flowers being on the "altar." There is a small side-chapel on the south side of the church, with an altar, candles, cross, and flowers. Morning Prayer takes place at half-past ten on Sundays, and the sermon—if the crude address which I heard may be so described—is introduced here instead of at the Holy Communion. This latter service takes place at half-past eleven, and at both services on Sunday there were good congregations. There was only one clergyman officiating, he being vested as for Mass, and having the help of two "servers" or "acolytes." Incense was not used, nor was any processional cross carried during any part of the service, though both "Crucifer" and "Thurifer" figure amongst the church officers whose names are given in the Parish Magazine. At the daughter church of the Transfiguration incense is, according to the *Tourist's Church Guide*, used. There were, of course, not the same changes of position nor ceremonial minutiæ as when a greater number of clergy officiate. There were no interpolations, except that of the *Benedictus qui venit* before, and that of the *Agnus Dei* after, the Prayer of Consecration, though both are, of course, serious enough. The prayer itself, as well as the whole service, was clearly audible throughout.

A "consecration" or "sacring" bell was rung at two points, together with the bell in the church tower; a bell was also rung at the *Ter Sanctus*. Although there was a large congregation not more than six persons communicated. The bowing to the altar on the part of both clergy and people was most pronounced, and the majority crossed themselves with great frequency. In the porch is a list of names of those on behalf of whom prayer is asked. This is classified into three divisions—for the sick, for those travelling, and for the departed—and under the latter heading there were nine names. I noticed that during the service there was a pause of some length, in the Prayer for the Church Militant, at the words "We also bless Thy Holy Name for all Thy servants departed this life in Thy faith and fear," and during the pause a very large number of the congregation prostrated themselves as far as the structure of the pews would permit. In the porch there was also a notice that two names, which were given, were to be added to the departed list of the Guild of All Souls. There is no mention of this Guild in the Parish Magazine, unless the cryptic announcement, "S. L. J. Guild Service," has any reference to it. It is not a little curious that in the magazine, while such familiar contractions as B.V.M. and C.B.S. are explained, the initials "S.L.J." are apparently supposed to require no interpretation.

The magazine gives the information that there is a local ward of the Confraternity of the Blessed Sacrament, and also a very full list of services; but it does not state anything about confession. This is also curious, because a small printed card, coyly affixed at the foot of a notice-board in the porch, furnishes a list of no fewer than seven occasions during the week on which the clergy attend in church for the hearing of confessions or for the giving of "ghostly counsel and advice," and gives the names of the clergy and their hours of attendance.

The recent and rapidly growing practice of having Children's Eucharists prevails here, though they are not expressly described as such, for the announcement of services for Sundays include the following :—

Holy Eucharist (Plain), 7 and 8 a.m.
      „   „   (Choral), *with Address to Children*, 9 a.m.
      „   „   „   11.30 a.m.

It is also announced that on Saturdays, except on festivals, there is Holy Eucharist for the faithful departed.

I went to one of the evening services during the week, but found a congregation of only eight persons. Two of the candles on the altar were lighted, and, of course, the seven sanctuary-lamps were burning. The smallness of the congregation may possibly have been caused by so many people being away on their holidays; but the extremely limited attendances at Matins and Evensong during the week is a striking commentary upon the alleged urgency of the demand on the part of the laity for daily services.

CHRIST CHURCH, CLAPHAM.

Vicar: REV. F. A. ORMSBY.
Patron: THE RECTOR OF CLAPHAM.

THE name of the Rev. Bradley Abbott has been a well-known one in the annals of Church life in South London. For forty years he laboured in one sphere, and when, nearly two years ago, he died, while on his holiday abroad, it was recognised by all parties in the locality that a good, if not a great, man had passed away. "Father" Abbott, as he was almost universally called, was Vicar of Christ Church, Clapham, a district lying between Larkhall Lane and Wandsworth Road. He built the church, and even to-day it is more often associated with his name than called by its legal designation. "Father" Abbott was one of the pioneers of advanced ritualism in South London. I remember attending the church nearly a quarter of a century ago, and being impressed by the ornateness of the service. "Fancy ritual" it was called then, even by some who were in sympathy with it.

It was not without interest, therefore, that I renewed my acquaintance with the church last Sunday morning, when I attended a choral celebration of the Holy Communion. The new Vicar was the celebrant, and I was able to see that, although there has been a change of incumbents, there has been a continuity of doctrine and ritual.

On entering the church one of the first things that caught my eye was a notice-board with the names of deceased persons for whom prayer was desired. In an almost equally conspicuous position was the announcement that the Vicar and his senior curate attend on certain evenings of the week to hear confessions. Passing up the church I noticed the side-chapel with a highly-decorated altar, candles, flowers, crucifix, and tabernacle being prominent. There was a solitary lamp burning before the altar, thus denoting that the Blessed Sacrament was reserved there; and as choir and clergy and some members of the congregation passed before it they bowed to it. Thus at the very outset one found evidence of

1. Prayers for the Dead,
2. Auricular Confession, and
3. Reservation of the Sacrament

being taught and practised at the church.

The celebration itself provided other instances of illegalities which could not but distress a moderate-minded Churchman. It is, however, only fair to add that it was rendered with care, reverence, and dignity throughout, and the music (Weber in E flat) was excellently performed. The service of Matins was over shortly before eleven, and after the Vicar and choir had retired the sacristan came in to prepare the altar for Mass. (I am perfectly entitled to use the word "Mass," for it was used by the Vicar in his sermon, and I find it also in the Parochial Report, p. 25.) Six tall candles and two smaller ones on or above the altar were lighted, as well as two standard candles, one on either side of the altar. The congregation, which at Matins had been small, had by this time greatly increased; but the church was not by any means full at any part of the service. The children from the school occupied the south aisle.

The organ pealed forth a grand march, and the choir, headed by a cross-bearer wearing a violet cassock, short surplice, and white gauntlets, and bearing aloft a processional cross, emerged from the vestry, and passing through the side-chapel entered the chancel through the gates. When all were in their places the celebrant, vested in a green chasuble and wearing a biretta, entered the sanctuary from a door on the south side. He was preceded by two young men carrying lighted candles (who afterwards acted as servers), and was attended by two boys, very diminutive in size, wearing short surplices and what looked like white kid gloves. An Introit was sung as the priest, reverently removing his biretta and bowing as he approached, took up his position before the altar. The little boys handed him the censer, and he duly censed the altar. Then moving to the south corner, and still facing eastwards, the priest began the Communion Office. His voice was audible throughout the service. He turned to the people as he read the Commandments, but he resumed his position, facing eastwards, for the Prayer for the Queen, the Collect for the Day, and the Epistle. Then the choir sang a Gradual or a Sequence, or both, the Service Book was moved by one of the servers to the north side of the altar, the priest censed the Gospel Book, and this ceremony over he read the Gospel. The Creed was sung to an elaborate setting, the priest and his servers returning to seats on the south side of the sanctuary after the first few sentences.

Towards the close of the Creed the priest came from his seat and made his way unattended to the pulpit. He had divested himself of his chasuble, and was wearing an extraordinary-looking long white vestment with close-fitting sleeves; his green stole was crossed in front; he had a white girdle round his waist; and he also wore his biretta—presenting altogether an almost grotesque appearance. The sermon, however, was an excellent one. It dealt with the temptations that beset people in their business life, their social life, and their religious life, and showed that it was only the Redeemer who could effectually succour those who are tempted. Except for a chance expression as to confession, it might have been preached with acceptance to an Evangelical congregation.

Returning to the sanctuary the priest resumed his chasuble, and took up his position before the altar. An offertory sentence was said and a hymn sung during the collection in the body of the church, while at the altar the priest was preparing the elements for consecration. Incense was again freely used. This time one of the little boys advanced down the chancel and censed the choir and also the people. The service then proceeded in the ordinary course, except that the priest *stood* during the Confession, whereas the rubric directs him to kneel, and that he made the sign of the cross at the word "pardon" in the Absolution. The sacring bell was rung during the singing of the *Sanctus*, and priest and people bowed low. The *Benedictus* was sung before the Prayer of Consecration, which was afterwards read by the priest amid circumstances of some pomp. Incense was used, the sacring bell and the bell in the tower were rung three times, the priest genuflected before the consecrated elements, he elevated the host and the chalice above his head, and many of the people in response bowed down in an attitude of adoration. At the close of the Prayer the *Agnus Dei* was sung. The music seemed to be more than usually long, and the priest meanwhile was constantly bowing and genuflecting before the consecrated elements, and (I presume) communicating himself. During the singing of the *Agnus* an aged lady who had been sitting with a companion in the front row of the seats in the south aisle (where the school children were sitting) passed through the side-chapel and, entering the chancel by the priests' door on the south side, knelt at the rails; and the priest, evidently aware of her presence, although he could not see her approach, as he had his back to the people, turned round and communicated her, and quickly returned to the altar. In spite of the large congregation present there were no other communicants. No sort of pause was made for intending communicants to approach the altar, neither did the priest even turn round in an attitude of invitation. The service, which had been to all intents and purposes a Mass, was then quickly brought to a close. After the Blessing had been pronounced the hymn "I heard the voice of Jesus say" was sung, during which the priest performed the ablutions, the two candles which were carried before him as he entered the sanctuary at the beginning of the service were relighted, and carried in front of him as he returned through the side door to the vestry. The choir remained in their stalls to sing the *Nunc Dimittis;* this over, they left the choir in the order in which they had entered it. The Vicar quickly disrobed, for in a moment or two he emerged from the vestry wearing cassock and biretta, and stationing himself at the door at the west end shook hands with the congregation as they dispersed.

I make no comment upon the use of illegal vestments, nor upon any of the "fancy ritual," but the conduct of the service as a whole was plainly antagonistic to the spirit of worship in the Church of England. Three points only need to be mentioned in proof of this:

1. Adoration of the Elements.
2. No reasonable opportunity given for intending communicants to receive the Sacrament.
3. Absence of the minimum number of communicants required by the rubric.

AT ALL SAINTS', LAMBETH.

Vicar: REV. F. G. LEE, D.D.
Patron: THE VICAR OF ST. JOHN'S, WATERLOO ROAD, S.E.

THE services at All Saints', Lambeth, where the Rev. F. G. Lee, D.D., has been Vicar for thirty-two years, have long been notorious. The following report of a choral celebration of Holy Communion fully justifies the reputation which the church has obtained.

The district of All Saints', Lambeth, embraces some of the most squalid parts of South London. The church is situated in a by-street just off the thoroughfare widely known as the Lower Marsh, which runs from Waterloo Road to Westminster Bridge Road. The Vicar—the Rev. Dr. Lee—who has been there a great many years, has for a long time been associated with the "Catholic revival," and in regard to both doctrine and ritual it has been always understood that you could be sure of the "correct thing" at All Saints'. Moreover, Dr. Lee is one of the clergymen connected with the Order of Corporate Reunion. It is commonly reported that he looks upon Rome with a tender eye, and there is reason to believe that whatever doubts certain advanced clergy may have about the validity of their Orders, he has absolutely none about his own. It is, too, an interesting indication of the Vicar's sympathies that amongst the numerous cards at the west end of the church, begging you of your charity to pray for the repose of the

All Saints', Lambeth 51

soul of So-and-so, is one bearing the name of Cardinal Newman.

I do not know for how long All Saints' has been notorious for its "Catholic" services, but certainly the church was never built for a display of advanced ritual. It does not even possess a chancel; it has an apse instead. But any difficulty on this score has been removed by the erection across the nave of the church of a wooden screen of slender build, and surmounted by a crucifix and six candles. Within this screen sat choir and clergy. The choir was not a large one, but two of the men had brass instruments, so there was a good volume of sound. Contrary to general custom the clergy seats are at the east end of the stalls farthest away from the people. The High Altar is in the apse. Just below the steps leading to the High Altar there are three chairs, and behind them a large reading-desk, all placed so that anyone using them would be facing eastwards. There are two side-altars, and the whole appearance of the east end seemed rather to suggest that of a not too well-kept Roman Catholic chapel. The church itself looked dirty and decayed; but it is clear that other things at All Saints' need restoring besides the fabric.

The church seats something like 2000 people, for there are deep galleries along either side and at the west end; but on Sunday morning last, when I was present at Matins and at the choral celebration, it was almost empty. The congregation consisted of two men (one of whom was myself), eight women, and seven children, and of these one woman and two children left the church during the progress of the service. It is quite evident, therefore, that whatever may be the influence of Catholic doctrine and high ritual amongst the leisured classes of the West, they have no power to attract the masses of this parish. It was a melancholy sight—a congregation of seventeen in a church capable of holding 2000, and Dr. Lee, standing before the High Altar, attired in gorgeous vestments and celebrating the Communion to the accompaniment of organ, trumpets, and choir.

Of the service itself not much need be said. It followed the lines with which the reader is by this time familiar, except that the ritual was less ornate than that to be seen at the West End. But seeing that the offertories are so small in amount it is obvious that the strictest economy must be practised. Dr. Lee announced from the altar that on the previous Sunday they amounted to one shilling in the morning and two shillings at night, and threepence at a celebration during the week.

For the celebration there were four candles lighted at the High Altar. Dr. Lee was the celebrant. He wore a green chasuble, and was attended by a lad who acted as server. The Introit having been sung, he began the service at the north side of the altar, only crossing to the south side for the Collect and Epistle, both of which he read facing eastwards. He recrossed to the north side for the Gospel, but before he read it he bowed towards the elements. The sermon—a very short one—was preached by the curate, who, as he passed the small altar in the north aisle on his way to and from the pulpit, ostentatiously bowed towards it. But there was no other evidence of the Reserved Sacrament being there. During the offertory hymn Dr. Lee went to the south corner of the altar and washed his fingers with some water that was brought to him by the server from the credence table, and wiped them with a towel. Returning to the centre of the altar he read the Prayer for the Church Militant, adding to the clause, "And we also bless Thy Holy Name for all Thy servants departed this life in Thy faith and fear," the words "Particularly those for whom we are bound to pray." During the singing of the *Sanctus* the sacring-bell was rung three times by the server, and the celebrant bowed his head over the elements. The Prayer of Consecration was said with the accompaniments usual at such churches—the *Benedictus* was sung as a preliminary to it; during its recital the sacring-bell was rung at the words "This is My Body," and again at the words "This is My Blood"; the host was elevated and the celebrant genuflected before the consecrated elements; and at the close the *Agnus Dei* was sung. There were no communicants. Dr. Lee turned to the people with the paten in his hand, but no one approached, and he resumed the service. It seems strange that when the service is merely a Mass and not a Communion that the celebrant should not hesitate to use the prayer which contains the words "humbly beseeching Thee, that all we, who are partakers of this Holy Communion . . ."; but Dr. Lee used it on Sunday as I have heard other priests use it under precisely similar circumstances. The service was then brought to a close. In pronouncing the blessing Dr. Lee made the sign of the cross three times at the mention of the Trinity. A hymn was sung while the ablutions were being performed, and the service finally concluded with the singing of the *Nunc Dimittis*.

It is hardly necessary to comment upon a service of this kind; it carries with it its own condemnation.

ST. MARY MAGDALENE, BRADFORD.

Vicar; REV. G. E. REDHEAD.
Patrons: THE TRUSTEES.

A VISITOR to Bradford during the Church Congress sent the following account of a High Celebration at the Church of St. Mary Magdalene:—

There have been lately published in the *Record* some reports of services at "advanced" churches in the Metropolis. I now venture to send you a description of a choral celebration of the Holy Communion as I saw it on Sunday at the Church of St. Mary Magdalene, Bradford; and from this report your readers will see that many of the objectionable practices, which have been noted in London churches, were re-enacted at St. Mary Magdalene. I hasten, however, to say that, so far as I could see, the Sacrament is not reserved there, and that on Sunday there were the bare number of communicants required by the rubric; but in all other respects the service was conducted in a way that suggested the Mass rather than the simple Communion Office of the Church of England.

The church is the most "advanced" in Bradford; the Six Points are observed, though incense was not used last Sunday. It is situated in the district known as White Abbey, and the streets in the immediate neighbourhood are of a squalid character. But the ritualism of the service makes little impression on the poor people around, a very few of

St. Mary Magdalene, Bradford 55

whom were to be found in the church. The congregation—a very large one—was mainly composed of well-dressed people (one or two arrived in carriages), and their appearance suggested that they had come from outside the parish rather than from within it. The church is a handsome Early English building, and the appointments at the east end showed that there is no lack of money to keep things up to the mark. The fine oak screen is a handsome piece of work, but above it there is a rood beam with a huge crucifix with figures on either side. There is no reredos, the space at the back being filled by coloured curtains, forming an artistic background. The High Altar, which is approached by a series of steps, was on Sunday last effectively arranged. A large brass cross stands on a ledge above it, and on the ledges below were six candles—three on either side—and a luxurious display of flowers. On the altar itself there were the familiar altar cards containing, it is understood, the prayers for the private use of the priest, and the frontal was of sage-green beautifully embroidered with gold trimming. Burning before the altar were seven red lamps, and at the bottom of the steps were two huge standard candles. There is a side-altar, but with this we are not now concerned.

The service was timed to begin at 10.45, and just before that time a sacristan or server appeared to light the candles. He was dressed in a scarlet cassock, and over it he wore a tight-fitting white vestment edged with lace and a scarlet girdle round his waist. When all was ready the choir of men and boys, and two clergy, one of whom was Dr. Cobb, of the E.C.U., marched up the church from the west end, and immediately afterwards the procession of the celebrant entered from a vestry at the east end. The cross-bearer came first, and he was followed by two little boys and two men (who acted as servers), all of them in scarlet cassocks, white vestments, and (except the cross-bearer) scarlet girdles;

and finally came the celebrant, wearing a biretta and what are called the eucharistic vestments, his chasuble being of sage-green, elaborately decorated with gold braid, to match the altar frontal. The hymn " As pants the hart for cooling streams " was sung as the celebrant and his two servers in the scarlet cassocks approached the altar. They made obeisance as they did so, the celebrant also removing his biretta. The priest took up a central position before the altar, and the two servers stood a step or two below, one on either side. As a display—I do not mean to use the word offensively at all—the scene at the east end was now impressive. The altar was brilliant with light (even the credence table had two lighted candles on it), and the varied colours of the vestments were most striking.

The service then began, and followed much the same lines as those already described in these pages. The priest read in an audible voice throughout. He read the Epistle, facing the people, one of the servers holding the book in front of him. The reading of the Gospel was more ceremonially performed. The priest passed to the north side of the altar; one of the servers standing just below held the book, or rather supported it on his forehead, while the cross-bearer, holding the cross aloft, and the two little boys grouped themselves behind the server who was holding the book. At the close they returned to their places, and the Creed was sung, the priest standing before the altar throughout. It was curious to note, however, that the choir, which turned to the east at the Doxology in the hymn, did not turn for the Creed. But at the *Incarnatus* clergy, choir, and congregation knelt down while the words were sung as a solo by a choir-boy. After the Creed came the sermon. Dr. Cobb was the preacher, and he spoke with some eloquence on Pharisaism, having a fling, towards the close, at those who go to church to criticise services which they regarded as idolatrous, but which were really only the outward expression of the true devotion of the heart. The offertory was collected during the singing of the hymn "For all Thy saints who from their labours rest," and then the service proceeded. Contrary to the practice at most other churches the people stood for the Comfortable Words, the *Sursum Corda*, the Preface, and the *Sanctus*. The *Benedictus* was then sung, and the priest afterwards read the Prayer of Humble Access. When he read the Prayer of Consecration the two servers, who had been kneeling below, one at either end, approached to the centre and knelt together, immediately behind the priest, and bowed their heads apparently to the ground. At the words of consecration the wafer and the chalice respectively were elevated, and many of the congregation bowed their heads in response.

The *Agnus Dei* was sung and the priest continually genuflected before the elements; his private devotions at this time seemed to be accompanied by a continual making of the sign of the cross over the elements. Four persons communicated, and thus the letter of the rubric was complied with; but whether the spirit of it was not grossly and flagrantly violated is another matter. The rubric runs thus:

¶ *And if there be not above twenty persons in the Parish of discretion to receive the Communion; yet there shall be no Communion, except four (or three at the least) communicate with the Priest.*

There were certainly "above twenty persons" in the church. The congregation must have numbered nearly 500, yet only four communicated. After the Blessing (during the recital of which the priest made the sign of the cross) the hymn "Fight the good fight with all thy might" was sung, and the priest performed the ablutions. He was afterwards escorted from the sanctuary to the vestry by the cross-bearer, the servers, and the acolytes. The choir afterwards retired, and the service closed.

The reader may be left to judge whether such a service is in accordance with the spirit and intention of the Communion Service in the Church of England.

ST. JOHN THE EVANGELIST, UPPER NORWOOD.

Vicar: REV. W. F. LATROBE-BATEMAN.
Patrons: THE TRUSTEES.

THE Church of St. John the Evangelist, Upper Norwood, recently acquired a certain notoriety on account of the allegations made by the Rev. R. B. Ransford, the Vicar of the adjoining parish, that the Sacrament is reserved there, and that whenever it is required it is carried about the parish for administration to the sick. Moreover, it was affirmed that the Vicar asked the people to do reverence to it whenever they might meet it. These allegations have not been denied by the Vicar, although he has offered some explanation of the nature of the permission given to him by the late Archbishop Benson in regard to Reservation for the sick. I attended a choral celebration of the Holy Communion at this church last Sunday, and some account of the service may not be without interest at the present juncture.

But, first of all, a word or two about the church. It is in the Auckland Road, Upper Norwood—a pleasantly-situated suburban district about eight miles out of London. The population in the immediate neighbourhood of the church consists of well-to-do villa residents, and the handsome church, no less than its elaborate appointments, suggests that there is plenty of money to be had; although I notice in the Parish Magazine that the Vicar says he cannot provide "a fourth priest" "unless we can secure a grant for the stipend of the same from one of the Church Societies." The church, which is a very capacious one, was crowded for Matins at 10.45; but there was a great exodus at the close. The number who attended the choral celebration at noon was much less than at Morning Prayer, but it was still considerable—about 300, the great majority of whom were women. The interior of the church is very impressive. There is a massive stone screen surmounted by figures of the Four Evangelists, and above them, hanging from the roof, is a very large gilt cross. The reredos behind the High Altar contains in relief representations from the life of our Lord, the Crucifixion filling the centre-piece. There is a large red lamp burning before the altar, denoting that the Sacrament is reserved there. I was puzzled about this, for at first I could not see the tabernacle in its customary place, but a moment or two later my eye lighted upon it in a corner on the south side of the altar. There is a large side-chapel with an elaborately-decorated altar having a gilt triptych over it, and three red lamps burning in front of it. On the wall in the north transept there is a massive marble slab with a crucifix in high relief. There is also a small crucifix on the pillar by the pulpit. Two banners with embroidered pictures were resting against the screen; on one was the Good Shepherd, and on the other the Virgin and Child, this last bearing the inscription *Sancta Maria Mater Dei*. Shortly before twelve a server came in and lighted two of the four candles on the altar and the two standard candles on either side. The arrangement of the altar was more simple than at some other churches.

The choir and one clergyman passed to their places in the chancel, and immediately afterwards the celebrant, preceded by the cross-bearer holding aloft a brass cross, and attended by two servers, came in. The priest wore the Eucharistic

St. John the Evangelist, Upper Norwood

vestments, his chasuble being of red silk embroidered with gold trimming. An Introit was sung, and with profound obeisance the celebrant approached the altar. The service proceeded much on the lines of other services already described in these columns. There was, perhaps, rather less ostentation than at some other churches, but the varied attitudes of the celebrant, and indeed the general conduct of the service, suggested the doctrine of a Real Objective Presence in the elements. The priest read the Epistle facing eastwards, and immediately afterwards a Gradual was sung, during which the Gospel-book was moved to the north side of the altar. The priest appeared to kiss the book, and then he read the Gospel, facing almost due east. The Creed was sung to an elaborate setting. Many of the congregation knelt at the *Incarnatus*, and the priest bowed himself low over the altar. During the offertory hymn he prepared the elements, and before he returned to the centre of the altar he appeared to wash the tips of his fingers. The service then proceeded, the *Benedictus* being sung before the Prayer of Humble Access. During the prayer following the priest bowed his head right down to the altar after the words of consecration; he elevated the paten and chalice above his head, and the bell in the tower of the church was rung three times. The *Agnus Dei* was sung, and towards the close of it the young clergyman who was sitting in the choir put on a stole, and proceeded to the sacrarium to assist in the administration. As he approached the altar he made profound obeisance towards it. The celebrant turned round towards him and elevated the chalice; the clergyman genuflected before it, and on rising from his knee took it with his hands and elevated it before the celebrant, who in his turn genuflected before it. This ceremony was repeated after the administration, before replacing the chalice on the altar. It was the clearest and most ostentatious act of adoration that I have ever seen. There were about fifteen communicants—all women—but it will not be forgotten that the congregation was a large one. Far the greater number of them, therefore, were non-communicating attendants. The celebrant pronounced the Blessing, facing the people, but at the mention of the name of the Second Person in the Trinity he turned his head, and in the most marked way bowed towards the elements on the altar, the significance of this act being apparent to everyone. A hymn was sung while the priest cleansed the vessels, and he then retired with his servers to the vestry. The choir afterwards left the chancel singing the *Nunc Dimittis*.

It may not be without interest to add that notice is given in the Parish Magazine of no fewer than six services to be held at St. John's on "All Souls'" Day, November 2nd (which is not in the English Calendar); and of one, a "Requiem," at the daughter church of St. Alban.

THE CHURCH OF THE HOLY REDEEMER, CLERKENWELL.

Vicar: REV. E. V. EYRE.
Patrons: THE TRUSTEES.

AN advertisement in the *Church Times* regarding some special services at the Church of the Holy Redeemer, Clerkenwell, attracted my attention, and as I had long heard of the advanced character of the ritual practised there, I determined to go and see for myself how some of the offices of the Church are rendered. The church is a comparatively new one, the special services of Sunday last being connected with the tenth anniversary of its consecration. The story goes—but I cannot vouch for its accuracy—that at the consecration of the church Dr. Temple, who was then Bishop of London, insisted on having a temporary platform erected to enable him to take the north end at the Holy Communion service, for the "altar" had been built so as to make that position impossible. Having now seen the church for myself, I can only express my surprise that the Bishop under any circumstances consented to consecrate it. It is built in the Italian style, and so closely resembles in its appointments a Roman church that a Protestant Churchman might well be excused if he mistook it for one of the buildings of the Italian Mission. As soon as you enter the church you are face to face with a massive baldachino supported by huge granite pillars, the dome being surmounted by a large gilt cross. Within this baldachino the altar has been erected, and on Sunday last it presented a gorgeous appearance. On the ledges above it there were twenty-eight candles of varying sizes and a profusion of white flowers tastefully arranged in expensive gilt vases, while in the centre there was a little box arrangement, which looked suspiciously like a pyx, and this was surmounted by a gilt crucifix. I hesitate to say that the Sacrament is reserved there, for although the tell-tale red lamp was burning before the altar when I entered the church, the light seemed to go out before the service was over. It was, however, noticeable that clergy, choir, and most of the congregation bowed towards the altar whenever they had occasion to pass before it. The baldachino is not built against the east wall, but in the body of the church, between the north and the south transepts. I did not penetrate into the mysteries of the space behind it, but from where I was sitting I could discern candles burning and a tapestry canopy reaching almost to the roof. I draw the conclusion, therefore, that there is an "altar" there, and that this part of the church is what is called in the Parish Magazine "The Lady Chapel."

The Dedication Festival began on October 13th, and Sunday last was called the "Day of General Communion." I notice in the Parish Magazine that the Vicar says "the administrations will be at 6, 7, and 8." For the other services he refers the reader to the papers. Turning to one of these, I find that while the services at the hours he names are called "Holy Communion," the Holy Communion service at 11.15 which I attended is called "Solemn Eucharist," and there is no reference to administration. I leave the reader to judge the significance of the omission.

I reached the church on Sunday morning at 10.30, just in time for Morning Prayer and Litany. The congregation,

Church of the Holy Redeemer, Clerkenwell

apart from two rows of girls in charge of three "Sisters," was extremely small, and the service was gone through somewhat perfunctorily by two clergymen. There was no choir, and everything was read. At the close of this service, however, the church rapidly filled, and it is just that I should say that the congregation was a reverent and devout one. The school children were brought in by some "Sisters," and occupied the seats in the transepts. Shortly after 11 two servers in scarlet cassocks lighted the twenty-eight candles on the altar, and the scene was a brilliant one. Afterwards one of them brought in a richly embroidered chasuble and laid it on the altar. The reason for this appeared presently. As a preliminary to the service there was a procession of choir and clergy round the church, which was intended to be of an impressive character. It was headed by a young man bearing aloft a processional crucifix, and at intervals in the procession six banners were carried. Following the choir came the assistant clergy of the church and the preacher, while the priest who was about to celebrate brought up the rear. He wore a handsome cope and a biretta, and he was attended by two servers in scarlet cassocks and cottas. The procession started from the space behind the baldachino, and, singing a hymn meanwhile, came along the south aisle and up the centre aisle to the altar. The route was everywhere strewn with leaves of laurel, evergreens, and firs. The choir, clergy, and banner-bearers passed into the space before the altar and ranged themselves on either side in front of the baldachino, a few remaining outside to form an escort for the celebrant. As soon as he and his attendants passed in and made their way to the steps leading to the altar, the man with the crucifix took up a position just behind him and held the crucifix aloft, the choir-men grouped themselves round him, the banners were raised on high, and as a spectacle an imposing effect was produced. Those who were thus engaged remained in this position until the processional hymn was concluded, when they retired to their respective places, leaving the celebrant and his servers ready to proceed with the Communion Office. But before this could be done he must needs change his vestments, and, standing there before the altar, and in sight of the crowded congregation, one of the servers took the cope off the celebrant, and fetching the chasuble and its appendages from the altar, robed him in it.

The service now began. The celebrant having made obeisance towards the altar (he had removed his biretta previously) took up a position at the south side and began the Office. He kept very closely to the Prayer-book all through. Neither the *Benedictus* nor the *Agnus* was sung. Whether this is the usual practice or not at this church I cannot say. I should not be surprised if they were omitted in deference to the wishes of the Bishop, for I see in the Parish Magazine that the Vicar, speaking of "a practice at variance with the rules set before us in the Book of Common Prayer, which is our standard," says he hopes that in future such divergences will be corrected. "The Commandments and Prayer for the Sovereign will in future be said at all celebrations, the celebrant will kneel at the Confession, and there will be a greater exactitude in the performance of the 'Manual Acts.'" This, of course, is all to the good, and shows that recent remonstrances in regard to the way the Holy Communion is celebrated at some extreme churches have not been in vain. There was much less bowing during the Prayer of Consecration than I have often witnessed. I could see also by the motion of his arms that the celebrant was performing the Manual Acts, whereas at other times and in other churches the celebrant has bowed himself over the elements so as to make it impossible to see whether he was doing anything at all. The elevation of

Church of the Holy Redeemer, Clerkenwell

the elements, too, was only of the slightest, but the church bell was rung twice at the words of Consecration, and the servers, for some reason that I cannot fathom, lifted up the tail of the celebrant's chasuble. Incense was used during the Prayer of Consecration, but not by the celebrant. I smelt it before I could see it, but in a moment or so the smoke came towards the altar from the south side, and I conjectured that one of the servers was manipulating the censer out of sight. I could tell that a few communicants were expected, for I saw the celebrant carefully count the wafers as he put them on the paten; and after the Prayer of Consecration one of the assistant clergy put on a stole, and, having bowed before the altar, went up to receive the chalice from the celebrant. Before taking it, however, he genuflected before it, repeating the performance when, after the administration, he returned it to the celebrant. The act of adoration was clear and unmistakable. There were six or seven communicants, and most of them were old people. Yet in the church there was a large congregation.

Behind the pulpit there is a crucifix. The sermon was preached by the Rev. L. Wainwright, Vicar of St. Peter's, London Docks. He put his stole on in the pulpit, having first reverently kissed it, and invoked the Trinity, making the sign of the cross meanwhile. He preached from the Gospel for the Day a very plain, practical, homely sermon, just suited to the intelligence of his congregation. Incidentally he spoke of the blessings of confession which the people at that church enjoyed. Here, perhaps, it may be convenient to refer to what the Vicar says on the same subject. In his letter in the Parish Magazine he speaks of "the immense treasure of grace opened to penitent sinners in the Ordinance of Confession"; and it is stated that he "attends in church on Saturdays from 8 to 9.30 p.m., at other times by appointment," and that one of the other clergy "attends on Thursdays at 11 a.m. and 7.30 p.m., and on Saturdays at 7.30."

Within a short distance of this church the Smithfield Martyrs were burned, and I could not help asking myself as I witnessed the service I have described, Was it for this hat they gave their bodies to the stake?

ST. AGNES', KENNINGTON PARK.

Vicar: REV. ALFRED HOLLAND.
Patrons: THE TRUSTEES.

THE Church of St. Agnes', Kennington Park, is situated within the proverbial stone's-throw of the residence of the Bishop of Rochester. It was built in 1874, and from the very first it has been a centre of advanced doctrine and ritual. The Rev. T. B. Dover was the first Vicar, and on his preferment to another living some four years ago St. Agnes' was offered to a well-known London clergyman, who, before accepting it, proposed to moderate the ritual. The trustees (of whom the Bishop of Lincoln is one) would not listen to him, and he declined the living. The present Vicar was then appointed. I have never attended service there before, so that I am unable to say whether any alterations have been made by the present Vicar; but if so I should hardly think they can have been of a moderating character, for a service more out of harmony with the spirit and principles of the Prayer-book than was that at St. Agnes' on Sunday morning I have seldom witnessed. It was called on the church board " High Celebration."

The church was used long before its internal decoration was finished. This has been proceeded with at intervals, and the most noticeable addition to the structure since its consecration is the oak screen, rood loft, and rood. The massive crucifix, with the figures on either side of it, is very prominent, and suggests the inquiry whether a faculty was obtained for this erection. There are two side-chapels with altars, and in that on the north side of the choir the Sacrament is reserved. I gather from a letter in the Parish Magazine that this is done ostensibly for the purpose of communicating the sick, but the fact undoubtedly is that the Sacrament has become an object of adoration on the part of the people attending the church. On Sunday morning last I saw several of them bowing to it, and others (amongst these one of the officials of the church) ostentatiously genuflecting before it.

The "High Celebration" began at eleven o'clock, at which time the choir entered the chancel. The hymn "Holy, Holy, Holy, Lord God Almighty" was sung, and the celebrant's procession entered. It was headed by two lads vested in tight-fitting white vestments, with girdles round their waists and what looked like a muffler arrangement round their necks, and each carried a lighted candle. There were also two smaller boys similarly attired, while the celebrant was attended by his two curates as deacon and subdeacon respectively. All three clergy were vested in chocolate-coloured chasubles. They approached to the steps of the High Altar and bowed low before it. They afterwards went to the altar itself, and the celebrant, supported on either side by his curates, censed the altar. There were four candles burning, but the acolytes kept theirs alight as well for uses which will be afterwards explained. The celebrant began the service at the south side of the altar, facing eastwards, the deacon and subdeacon standing on the steps below him, one behind the other, in a slanting direction. It would serve no useful purpose to record the many and varied movements of this trio, although at times their performances presented a positively grotesque appearance. I prefer rather to invite attention to more important matters connected with the service.

During the reading of the Commandments the lads with the candles moved from side to side, until at length they came out of the choir, carrying their lighted candles in their hands. They returned in a moment or two, escorting another lad, similarly attired and with a green cape over his shoulders, who brought in the elements. The Epistle was read by the subdeacon, who came right down to the chancel gates for the purpose. The Epistle ended, the singing of a hymn was interpolated, during which the deacon and the subdeacon, accompanied by the lads with the candles, came rather more than half-way down the choir on the north side and grouped themselves in position. The subdeacon held the Gospel Book, and the deacon then read the Gospel, facing northwards in the direction of the chapel where the Sacrament is reserved. The Gospel over, the clergy returned to the altar and the lads to their former positions, and the Creed was sung. The three clergy, however, retired to the south side of the chancel before it was concluded, and in a minute or two the subdeacon, having divested himself of his chasuble, ascended the pulpit and preached the sermon.

Immediately after the sermon the preacher returned to the sacrarium, resumed his chasuble, and the "three men in red" were again very much *en évidence* at the altar. During the singing of the offertory hymn incense was again used, the celebrant, choir, and people being censed. The elements having been prepared, the celebrant washed the tips of his fingers and resumed the service. I noticed that he stood during the Confession, although the rubric directs him to kneel. The singing of the *Benedictus* was interpolated just before the Prayer of Humble Access. As soon as the priest began the Prayer of Consecration several of the congregation, particularly on the women's side, crouched down and remained so until the prayer was finished. It was not possible to see the Manual Acts, for the celebrant bent his body over the elements, and the actual words of consecration were absolutely inaudible. The celebrant elevated the wafer and the chalice respectively above his head, and the church bell was rung. The *Agnus Dei* was then sung, and towards the close of it I noticed a young lady approach the rails through the chapel on the north side, and in a moment or so the celebrant turned round to give the chalice to the deacon. But he first of all elevated it, and the deacon and some of the acolytes near fell at once on to their knees as though they had seen a vision. The celebrant, holding up the wafer, went to the rails, followed by the deacon carrying the chalice, and, the young person having been communicated, both clergy returned quickly to the altar, and the service proceeded. There was thus only one communicant, although the church was full of people. After the Benediction a hymn was sung, during which the priest performed the ablutions, and the service was brought to a close.

This is a sample of the service which is held every Sunday morning within two or, at the most, three minutes' walk of the residence of the Bishop of the diocese.

ST. ANSELM'S, STREATHAM.

THE Church of St. Anselm, Streatham, is situated in Coventry Park, quite close to Streatham Station. I have often passed it, but the notices on the church board look so innocent that I had never realised what extraordinary services are sometimes performed there. Recently, however, a copy of the Parish Magazine came into my hands, and there, to my amazement, I saw in the announcements that there is a "Celebration for Faithful Departed" once every week. I accordingly went to the church on Monday morning last at 8 a.m., the time announced for one of these services. A congregation of four—three ladies and one man—were seated in the side-chapel, but there was no clergyman, and, as a matter of fact, it must have been nearly half-past eight before the service began. But the congregation had not increased meanwhile. This chapel is called "The Lady Chapel," and above the altar there is a picture of the Virgin and Child. On the altar-ledge there are a crucifix and two candles. These latter were lighted by the clergyman himself, there being no server, and he afterwards retired to robe. When he emerged again from the vestry he was wearing a massive black chasuble trimmed with yellow silk and carrying the elements, the coverings for which were also of black and yellow silk. Having placed the elements on the altar he retreated a few steps, bowed before them, crossed himself, said some private prayers, and then took up his position at the south side of the altar, facing east, to begin the service. He used a service-book which looked suspiciously like the *Canon of the Mass*. He read the service in a very low voice, and at so alarming a pace that it was difficult to follow him. The Commandments were omitted, and after the collect for the day he interpolated a collect from the Office for the Burial of the Dead. He ignored the Epistle and Gospel appointed for the day, and read in their place—for the Epistle a short passage from 1 Cor. xv. and for the Gospel a short passage from (I think) St. John, but I could not catch the reference. The offertory was collected by the young man in the congregation, who afterwards retired—evidently to catch his train for town, as the service was late. After the offertory the priest said, "Let us pray for the dear departed." There was then a considerable pause, during which he was evidently saying secret prayers. The Prayer for the Church Militant followed, and the service proceeded. During the Confession the priest rested his elbows on the altar and bent his body over the elements—an attitude he also assumed when reading the *Sanctus*. Before the Prayer of Consecration there was another pause. He kissed the altar, and, from the way he moved his hands and arms about, and turned over the page of the book, he was evidently again engaged in secret prayers. When at length he read the Prayer of Consecration he did so in a very low tone, and bowed himself so closely over the elements that it was impossible to see the Manual Acts. After the words of consecration he elevated the wafer and the chalice respectively and ostentatiously genuflected before them, and the bell in the tower was tolled. After the prayer there was again another long pause, and finally the priest turned round, muttered a single sentence, which I could not catch, made the sign of the cross with the wafer, turned back again, and resumed the service without giving anyone the opportunity of communicating, even if they desired to do so. The Lord's Prayer and the Collect

St. Anselm's, Streatham

following having been said, the three people in the chapel retired, having first genuflected to the altar, and the priest was left alone at the altar. He duly performed the ablutions, and so this "Celebration for Faithful Departed" was concluded. In what way it differed from a Mass for the Dead I have not yet been able to discover.

It may be worth while to add that on leaving the church I found by the north door a notice giving the "Hours for Confessions."

ST. MICHAEL AND ALL ANGELS, LADBROKE GROVE.

ST. MICHAEL'S CHURCH is one of those in which special services were recently held in honour of the distinctly Roman Festival of Corpus Christi, an account of which will be found on pages 1–5. The Vicar, Prebendary Denison, was not, however, among those who afterwards signed the letter promising to respect the wishes of the Bishop of London in the matter of conformity to the Prayer-book.

Morning Prayer and Litany began on Sunday last at 10.30, at which time four people were in church, and this number was only increased by about seven during the service, though the wet weather and the holiday season may account in part for so remarkably small a congregation. There was no choir and no singing; two clergy conducted the service, one acting as clerk to repeat the responses. The *Venite*, the Psalms, and the *Te Deum* were read very quickly, the two clergy taking alternate verses. After Morning Prayer one of the clergy left the chancel, and kneeling down in the middle aisle said the Litany at a rapid pace, both services having to be got through at least within the half-hour. As a matter of fact the whole occupied rather less than twenty-six minutes, leaving about five minutes as an interval before the Communion Service. During this interval an acolyte lit six of the candles on the High Altar.

The church is large and open, a chancel being made by

St. Michael and All Angels, Ladbroke Grove 77

the erection of a low stone wall closed in by wrought-iron gates. There is a side-chapel, which is described in the Parish Magazine as the "Lady Chapel." This contains an altar, with a large brass cross and a number of candles upon it, and before it a sanctuary-lamp was burning, indicating that the Sacrament was reserved. On one of the walls of this chapel is a picture of the Virgin and Child, before which at certain times lighted candles are placed after the manner of Roman Catholic churches.

The "Stations of the Cross" are hung round the walls of the church, but all except two are merely oleographs without frames. The two exceptions are framed oil paintings, each surmounted by a gilt cross; a third painting is ready, but, according to the Parish Magazine, is waiting for the gift of a frame, which is a somewhat expensive consideration.

The High Altar is surmounted by a lofty canopy, and is literally crowded with candles. It has a large brass cross with what bears a close resemblance to a tabernacle at its base, and there are five sanctuary-lamps burning before it.

Punctually at eleven o'clock the clergy, choir, and acolytes entered the church and proceeded to the choir, the six acolytes being in red cassocks, cottas, and zuchettos, or skull-caps. Two of the acolytes carried candles, and one a thurible or censer. The service was not preceded by either the Asperges or Antiphon, but began with the Lord's Prayer, and was, so far as the words are concerned, conducted according to the Prayer-book. Two hymns were sung—one before and one after the Prayer of Consecration—in place of the *Benedictus qui venit* and the *Agnus Dei*. In the "Preface," at the words "Holy, holy, holy, Lord God of Hosts," the sacring bell was rung, and this bell, together with that in the tower, was rung twice during the Prayer of Consecration. At the words "This is My Body" the acolytes elevated the candles which they bore, while incense was freely used both here and at other parts of the service. The Gospel was read towards the north-east, the clouds of incense rendering the minister almost invisible. There was only one celebrant vested as for Mass, but this was possibly on account of the general exodus of clergy from London during August. During this service there were between fifty and sixty persons present, but of these only four communicated. No invitation was given to the congregation, the clergyman at the altar remaining with his back to the people; and it seemed as if no communicants were expected, for one of the clergy, who knelt at the west end of the chancel facing east, hurriedly left his stall and went to the altar as the communicants passed him.

A short sermon was preached from 1 Cor. x. 13, "There hath no temptation taken you but such as is common to man." There was nothing remarkable about the sermon, the delivery of which made it difficult to follow in places.

The notice-board, besides announcing the days on which confessions are heard, states that Evening Prayer takes place daily at 5.30, and one evening during the week I went to the service. It was conducted in the Lady Chapel by two clergy, but with the exception of a lady, wearing the dress of some Sisterhood, I was the only person present. This, which is far from being an exceptional case, illustrates how little demand for daily service there is even in a parish where the duty of attending such services is of course inculcated.

ST. AUGUSTINE'S, SETTLES STREET, STEPNEY.

Vicar: REV. HARRY WILSON.
Patron: THE BISHOP OF LONDON.

THERE are a number of London churches which in ritual and doctrine are as "advanced" as any of those which are conspicuous for anti-Reformation teaching, and yet have not come prominently before the public. Of these St. Augustine's, Settles Street, E., is perhaps a fair example. The Vicar is among the number of those who signed the letter promising acquiescence in the wishes of the Bishop of London.

I have this week attended some of the services at St. Augustine's with the view of finding whether they were such as a casual inspection of the church a year or two ago led me to expect.

The *London Directory* states that services are held, besides other times, at ten o'clock and at eleven on Sunday mornings. I chose these two, thinking they would be Morning Prayer and Holy Communion respectively. I was surprised, however, to find that the earlier service was a "Children's Eucharist," which was celebrated by a clergyman vested as for Mass. A small service-book, called *The Children's Eucharist*, which appears to have been specially compiled for the use of this church, and has a Preface by the Vicar, was used. This book opens with a prayer to the

Holy Trinity: "Be pleased to accept this Holy Sacrifice of the Body and Blood of our Lord Jesus Christ, which we are about to offer unto Thee for Thy honour and glory," &c. It contains a number of hymns, among them the following, which is introduced before the Prayer for the Church Militant:—

> We offer gifts of Bread and Wine
> To Thee, O God most High;
> Send down on them Thy Holy Ghost,
> Descending from the sky.
>
> To make this offered Bread to be
> The Body of the Lord;
> The Wine within the sacred cup
> To be the Blood adored.
>
> With humble mind and contrite heart
> We come before Thy face.
> Let Mary and the saints on high
> Implore for us Thy grace;
>
> So shall Thy Holy Church on earth
> With every grace be blest;
> And so shall all the faithful dead
> Obtain eternal rest. Amen.

The directions in the book are all arranged to teach the doctrine of the Real Presence in its most literal and materialistic form, and the use of larger and heavier type at certain places impresses this teaching. The following notes come immediately after the Prayer of Consecration and before certain "Acts of Worship," which were obviously directed to the elements:—

"Now the Consecration is completed; now the Memorial has been made; now the bread has become the Body of Christ, and the wine has become the Blood of Christ, and where His Body and Blood are there is Jesus Christ Himself.

"Jesus Christ is here: worship Him with all your heart and soul."

There were scarcely fewer than sixty children present, ranging in age from about five to sixteen years, and they had evidently been carefully instructed, for they crossed themselves, bowed, and some prostrated themselves at various parts of the service with great precision.

During the service a clergyman came out of the vestry and seated himself in a chair in the south side of the church, and shortly afterwards a young lady went over, and kneeling down near him began apparently to confess. The clergyman at times spoke to her, and after a while she arose and went back to her seat. This confession was of course quietly and unostentatiously made so as not to disturb the other worshippers.

At the point where the sermon comes in a clergyman catechised the children for a short time. He said, among other things, that they were that day commemorating the Festival of the Holy Name, and that it was also the Vigil of the Assumption of the Blessed Virgin Mary. I could not quite understand this, as the black-letter festival of the Holy Name is in the Calendar for the previous Sunday, and the Assumption of the Blessed Virgin Mary is not in the Calendar at all. Great stress was laid upon the association together of the two names Mary and Jesus, and I could not but observe that the former always came first.

After the catechising the service proceeded. At the time for the people to communicate the celebrant turned to the congregation, and two girls, the only communicants, went up to the altar. The whole service lasted about forty minutes, leaving a considerable interval before the service at eleven.

By eleven o'clock a congregation numbering about 300 people had assembled. The church is not a large one, and it was, therefore, nearly filled. On the walls were hung the " Stations of the Cross," and also in two or three places small crucifixes at a height convenient for kneeling. A large crucifix was placed near the pulpit, and a number of banners

G

and a processional cross were in the chancel. There was a small Lady Chapel closed in with ornamental iron-work, and here a single sanctuary-lamp was burning, indicating the reservation of the Sacrament. The central, or High Altar, was raised several steps and surmounted by a lofty canopy. Six very large candles and a brass cross stood upon it, and across the chancel seven sanctuary-lamps were hung. At the hour of service the choir, acolytes bearing candles, and the clergy entered the church; but instead of Morning Prayer, which I expected at first when the candles on the altar were put out after the Children's Eucharist, though they were relighted just before eleven, the Mass was again celebrated. Morning Prayer, though announced on the notice-board for 10.15, must therefore have been said before the ten o'clock service, if at all.

The service was conducted in much the same way as those already described in these pages. There were genuflections, crossings, and innumerable changes of position on the part of the clergy and acolytes. The church bell was rung during the Prayer of Consecration; the *Agnus Dei* was sung at its close. There was the same use of incense and lighting of candles at the reading of the Gospel and other parts of the service. There were no communicants, and no opportunity was afforded for anyone to communicate; for though the celebrant turned round and made the sign of the cross with what appeared to be a wafer, he immediately resumed his position facing eastwards and continued the service. There was a procession round the church of clergy, acolytes, and choir, one acolyte swinging his censer, the five banners and the processional cross being used. The Collect, Epistle, and Gospel were not those appointed for the day, and I have been unable to discover whence they were obtained. The Collect for the Seventh Sunday after Trinity was certainly read, and so I believe was another, but it was not familiar

St. Augustine's, Settles Street, Stepney

to me. A member of the congregation whom I asked for information was equally unaware of the source of this part of the service.

One most objectionable feature of the service at this church was that at the Prayer of Consecration great numbers of the congregation—a considerable proportion and not merely a few eccentric individuals—prostrated themselves so that their foreheads actually touched the ground.

As it was announced that, the evening being the Vigil of the Assumption, the service would be of a special character, I went at night. There was a repetition of the procession of the morning, and the ordinary Evening Service was read. Of course incense was used at the *Magnificat*, of which on this occasion a special feature seemed to have been made. Other Psalms than those of the day were sung and different lessons were read, the first being taken from Solomon's Song iv., and the second from Revelation xii. By what authority was this done?

The sermon was preached from Judith xv. 8, and was chiefly a glorification of the Virgin Mary, based upon extensive quotations from legendary and traditional sources. The hymns used, of course, corresponded.

I reached the church a short time before the evening service began, and while I was waiting another confession was heard—this time from a young girl about sixteen or seventeen years of age.

Having seen the general character of the services on Sunday, I felt some curiosity as to those on the next day, when the Feast of the Assumption would be celebrated. This was not diminished when, after announcing that they would take place at 6, 7, 8, and 9.30 a.m., the minister requested the parents present to send their children fasting. I therefore went to the service announced for half-past nine. It proved to be another "Children's Eucharist." There were about thirty children, two or three teachers, and a few adults present. It was most difficult to hear the celebrant, and I could not catch all the words of the Collect, but it resembled the Proper Preface for Christmas Day. The Epistle was taken from the Canticles, and for the Gospel the *Magnificat* was read. The Commandments were not read, and there is no provision in the service-book for their being read. Possibly it was at St. Augustine's that this grave omission, of which Canon Gore has been told, and which he regards as greater than any ritualistic offence, took place. At the Prayer of Consecration three of the ladies prostrated themselves until their heads touched the ground, and they remained in that position for some three or four minutes. There were no communicants, though a distinct opportunity was afforded to anyone who might wish to partake. The service lasted only about half an hour, and during the greater part of the time I found it quite impossible to understand what the minister was saying, or even to be certain that he was speaking at all.

ST. CYPRIAN'S, MARYLEBONE.

IN a side street between Upper Baker Street and Dorset Square is one of the smallest and most curious churches in London. It is probably the smallest parish church in the Metropolis. The building was at one time a private house of very moderate dimensions, and the inscription, "St. Cyprian's Church," surmounting a large cross painted on the front, is the chief indication that it is even now other than a private house with a disproportionately large door.

The seating accommodation is very small; a congregation of about one hundred and fifty persons would fill the church; and it does not therefore lend itself to the scenic extravagances with which those who attend churches where "lawlessness" prevails are familiar. But the building is, of course, only a temporary one, and in about three years it is expected that Lord Portman will be able to dispose of a suitable site for a permanent church. It may therefore be interesting to note the indications which the present services afford of what the character of those in the new church will be. The chancel is raised some five or six steps above the floor of the building, and the altar some two or three above that. There are two large standard candlesticks, and on the altar a large brass cross, candlesticks, and flowers. The standard candlesticks are lighted for Evensong in broad daylight, and though the chancel is certainly dark they were of no use as illuminants, the diffused light being quite sufficient to enable the choir to read by.

Morning Prayer is said on Sundays at 10.30, and is followed at 11.15 by Choral Eucharist with Sermon. The *Tourist's Church Guide* states that on certain occasions incense is used. The occasion on which I attended the services of this church was not, however, one of these. The choir-boys were robed in purple cassocks and surplices, the men in black cassocks and surplices, while the officiating minister was vested as for Mass, though, as the congregation is evidently not a rich one, the vestments were of linen, and not of the costly embroidered materials used in wealthier churches. The Eastward Position was, of course, taken throughout the Communion Service, and all the candles were lighted. There were only two clergy, one being in deacon's orders; but the perpetual changing of position in relation to each other and to the Communion Table was practically the same as that where the more usual number of three prevails. The service was quite audible throughout, but, though there was a congregation of about sixty persons, there were *no* communicants. The *Benedictus qui venit* preceded the Prayer of Consecration, the *Agnus Dei* followed it, and the ceremony of the ablutions was performed at the close of the service.

Once a month there is a "Children's Eucharist," while the ordinary services include daily Eucharist, Matins, and Evensong, with three celebrations of the Holy Eucharist on Sundays. A great number of pictures hang round the church, and there is a brass with an inscription asking for prayers for the soul of Charles Gutch, priest, founder of the parish, and stating that for thirty years he laboured there. This memorial it is proposed to transfer to the new church. There are three Homes in connection with the parish—an Orphanage, a House of Mercy and Healing, and a Home for Aged Poor. The children belonging to these Homes were at one of the services I attended, in charge of ladies wearing the dress of some Sisterhood. The nature of the teaching which these children receive may be inferred from the character of the services in the church.

A "SUNG MASS" AT THE CHURCH OF ST. MARY AND ST. MARY MAGDALENE, BRIGHTON.

Vicar: REV. E. HEATH.
Patron: REV. A. D. WAGNER.

BRIGHTON, the Queen of Watering Places, has long been known as a stronghold of High Anglicanism, but I do not think it is at all generally understood to what extremes the movement has grown. The Eastward Position is now taken in twenty-five churches; altar candles are lighted in twelve churches; the mixed chalice is used in nine churches; the Eucharistic vestments are worn in seven churches; and incense is used in four churches. I believe also that the Sacrament is reserved in at least four churches; at any rate, I give the names of four where I saw the solitary lamp, which is always understood to denote reservation, burning before the altar.

> The Church of the Annunciation, Washington Street.
> St. Bartholomew's, London Road.
> St. Mary and St. Mary Magdalene, Bread Street.
> St. Michael and All Angels', Victoria Road.

On Sunday morning I attended service at one of these four churches, viz., that of St. Mary and St. Mary Magdalene, Bread Street—a humble-looking thoroughfare turning out of Church Street, and a few minutes from the sea. The surroundings are somewhat squalid, and the church itself, viewed from the outside, looks a ramshackle sort of building, while the interior wears a poverty-stricken appearance. It is a barn-like structure, and neither the colour-wash on the brick walls, nor the "Stations of the Cross," nor the other pictures, give much relief to the general dreariness of the place. I did not know exactly what sort of service I should find there; but the announcements I read in the porch and at the west end of the church prepared me for something very extreme. Amongst these announcements was one to the effect that "the eight o'clock Mass" would be discontinued on Sundays and Holy Days until further notice, there being no assistant-curate at the present time. Another was to the effect that at the eleven o'clock celebration no strangers would be allowed to communicate unless they had given verbal notice the day before; and immediately underneath this intimation was the extraordinary announcement that "the rule of the Catholic Church is" that no one shall communicate except when fasting, the only exception being in the case of sick persons. Then there were two notices about confessions. In one it was stated that the Rev. W. Stokes had kindly promised to be in church to hear confessions at such and such times, and in the other it was said that the Rev. E. Heath attends in church to hear confessions on such and such days. There was also a notice begging for prayers for a large number of dead persons whose names were given. One other notice calls for remark. The eleven o'clock service is called in the Parish Almanack "Choral Mass," and the MS. announcement of the hymns, music, &c., to be used on the Twenty-first Sunday after Trinity called it "Sung Mass."

We are often told of the power of "Catholic teaching and ritual" to get hold of the poor, but if one may judge from what I saw on Sunday I should say that it has lamentably failed in this district. The service of Morning Prayer was read at ten o'clock by the parson alone; there was no choir, and the congregation numbered exactly *two*—a lady and myself. For the "Sung Mass" the congregation was larger; but if we except the school children, who attended in force, I doubt very much whether there were more than eighty persons present. Moreover, it was patent from the Incumbent's discourse, which for courtesy's sake must be called a sermon, that the people have been very shabby in their offerings lately, and that even on Easter Day many of them must have limited their alms to one halfpenny or a penny.

Let me now give some account of this "Sung Mass." The choir (a few men and boys) entered the chancel from the vestry on the north side, and as soon as they were in their places the celebrant's procession came in from the south side. It was headed by two young boys carrying lighted candles, followed by two more boys, one carrying the censer and the other the incense. These little lads wore scarlet cassocks, cottas, and scarlet skull-caps. Then came two older lads—each wearing a close-fitting white vestment and a scarlet girdle—who acted as servers; and finally came the celebrant wearing a green chasuble (on the back of which was a representation of the Saviour on the Cross) and a biretta. When he arrived at the foot of the altar he bowed low towards it and removed his biretta. Before the altar a lamp was burning, and on a ledge above it there were six candles lighted. A hymn was here sung, during which the priest seemed to be engaged in private devotions, turning first to one lad and then to the other on either side of him. He afterwards turned round to the boy with the incense, and having prepared the censer and made the sign of the cross over it he censed the altar, and was afterwards censed himself by one of the boys. This done the lads returned to the vestry. The priest began the Communion Office at the north side, but crossed to the south side for the Collect and Epistle. He interpolated two collects after the Collect for the Day, and read the Epistle facing east. He returned to the north side for the Gospel, which he read amidst great ceremony. The boys with the candles held them aloft, and the boys with the incense returned to the sacrarium. The priest censed the Gospel Book and was himself censed. The Nicene Creed was then sung. After the Creed the priest, still vested in his chasuble, turned to the people and made various announcements (including in them that Wednesday was All Souls' Day), and then from the altar steps he preached his "sermon." It was on almsgiving, and never before have I heard a congregation so roundly rated for their deficiencies as were the poor people there assembled. The sermon otherwise calls for no remark, except to say that the preacher assumed that Adam offered various sacrifices unto God, even though it was not expressly stated, for, he gravely assured us, there was no Privy Council in those days to say that what was not ordered was forbidden.

The sermon over, the offertory was collected during the singing of a hymn. At this church they use a special hymn-book of their own, "printed for private circulation only." It is worthy of attention by the Bishop of Chichester.

The boys again brought in the incense, and it was freely used—altar, priest, choir, people, and even the offertory plate being censed. The celebrant rinsed his hands before proceeding with the service. The Prayer for the Church Militant followed. The invitation ("Ye that do truly") was said almost in a whisper, and the General Confession was recited by one of the youthful servers *alone*, neither priest, nor choir, nor people taking any part in it. During the *Sursum Corda* two of the younger boys brought two tall lighted candles in, and, kneeling down on a step below the servers, held them aloft, and they kept them in that position for some time. At the *Sanctus* the sacring-bell was rung three times. Immediately after the *Sanctus* the *Benedictus* was sung, and this was followed by the Prayer of Humble Access. A verse of a hymn was next interpolated, during which the boys removed their skull-caps preparatory to the Prayer of Consecration being said. During the prayer the choir were kneeling eastwards, and many of them bowed low, the heads of the boys almost touching the ground; and it was noticeable that several members of the congregation also bowed themselves. The prayer was said audibly, but the Manual Acts were hidden. The sacring-bell was rung three times at the words of consecration of the bread and wine respectively; the wafer and the chalice were elevated, and the priest afterwards genuflected before them. Incense was again used—one of the boys swinging the censer—during the Prayer of Consecration. After the prayer a hymn was sung, and this was followed by the singing of the *Agnus*, during which the priest made his communion, and the sacring-bell was again rung. At the time provided in the Prayer-book for the people's communion the priest simply turned round, made the sign of the cross with the wafer, turned immediately back again, and resumed the service to its conclusion. There were no communicants, but the hymn-book in use at this church provides a hymn for the use of the congregation as an "act of spiritual communion." I specially commend this hymn (No. 610) to the attention of the Bishop. The doctrine conveyed in it is hardly distinguishable from Transubstantiation.

After the Benediction a hymn was sung, during which the priest performed the ablutions. These over he bowed low before the altar, and his serving lads having arranged themselves in procession, the priest resumed his biretta and the lads their skull-caps, and so marched out of the sanctuary to the vestry, the choir following shortly afterwards to their vestry, and this "Sung Mass" concluded.

It may be well now to gather up the points upon which attention should be centred. I have made but little reference to the bowings, genuflections, and prostrations of this Massing priest, for they were so numerous that to do so would only be to weary the reader. But my report shows that at this church—

1. The Holy Communion is openly proclaimed to be a Mass.
2. The Sacrament is reserved.
3. No communicants are encouraged at the "Sung Mass."
4. Fasting Communion is said "to be the rule of the Catholic Church."
5. Incense is ceremonially used.
6. The Manual Acts are hidden.
7. The wafer and the chalice are elevated and adored.
8. There are various interpolations introduced into the Communion Office.
9. Auricular confession is encouraged.

These are things I discovered by a single visit to the church; no doubt a closer acquaintance with it would reveal other illegalities. I wonder if the Bishop of Chichester knows what is going on? and if so, what he thinks of it?

I should like to add a word as to what I saw at two other churches. At St. Bartholomew's, London Road, I found two confessional desks, each of which contains a crucifix. Amongst the announcements for November I noticed that there was to be—"Vespers of the Dead" at 8.15 p.m. on Tuesday, and that on Wednesday ("All Souls'" Day) there were to be no fewer than five celebrations of the Holy Eucharist. At the Church of the Annunciation I saw one confessional box and two spaces curtained off, apparently for the purposes of hearing confessions. There are also images in the church: one, of the Good Shepherd, over a table at the east end of the north aisle, on which are candles and flowers; and the other of the Virgin and Child, before which a blue lamp was burning, and on the pedestal there are candles and flowers. Again I venture to ask, Does the Bishop of Chichester know of these things? and if so, have they his approval?

THE TEACHING AT ST. ANSELM'S, STREATHAM.

THE article on p. 73 upon the services at this church excited much attention when it first appeared; but some copies of the Parish Magazine, *Leaves from our Diary*, show that what has been described is not a new departure at St. Anselm's. As long ago as December, 1891, there was a "celebration for faithful departed" every week; but, so far from any attempt being made to stop it, the clergy were encouraged to persevere in their lawlessness by a grant from the Rochester Diocesan Society in 1893. Moreover, the teaching was quite as advanced then as now. In the "Catechism Notes," which were running through the *Leaves* at that time, it is said that the Holy Communion is the greatest Sacrament because it "contains God Himself." Amongst the "other Sacraments" which "lead up to It" "*penance*" is named, and it is said that "*penance* cleanses us from all sins and makes us fit to receive It." Again, we learn that, in order to receive the Holy Communion worthily, we must prepare both our soul and our body:—

How can we prepare our *soul?*
By being in a state of grace.
What do you mean by being in a state of grace?
Free from mortal sin.
How can we be sure we are free from mortal sin?
By self-examination and confession.

The Teaching at St. Anselm's, Streatham 95

How must we prepare our bodies?
By keeping from all food and drink from 12 o'clock the night before.
Why must we be so particular to prepare our bodies?
1. It has been the invariable rule of the Church at all times and in all places.
2. We must do it from motives of reverence: Christ's Body should be the first Food that we receive.

Are people ever allowed to break this rule?
The Church allows the dying to receive not fasting.

Further, we learn that the Holy Eucharist is not a Sacrament only; it is also a Sacrifice:—

What is a Sacrifice?
The offering of a victim by a priest to God.
But did not Christ offer Himself once for all on the Cross?
Yes; that Sacrifice can never be repeated.
How, then, is the Holy Eucharist a Sacrifice?
Because it represents and sets forth the Sacrifice offered once for all on Calvary.
What are the four ends for which we offer the Holy Sacrifice?
1. Adoration.
2. Thanksgiving.
3. Propitiation.
4. Intercession.

Explain these four ends.
Adoration is to give to God supreme honour and glory.
Thanksgiving is gratitude for all His benefits both to body and soul.
Propitiation is that we may share in all benefits of His Passion.
Intercession is to plead the merits of Christ's death for ourselves and the whole world.

It is interesting to learn from these *Leaves* (January, 1892) the precise meaning attachable to the celebrant's vestments, and to the ceremonies observed at Holy Communion. Two Sundays are given up to the instruction of the young in these matters. We quote the Notes as follows:—

2ND SUNDAY AFTER CHRISTMAS, JAN. 3RD.

What is the Holy Eucharist besides a Sacrifice and a Sacrament?
It is also a memorial.

What is it a memorial of?
The Passion and Death of our Lord.

How do we do this?
Christ said, "This do in remembrance of Me." (St. Luke xxii. 19.)

How is this shown in the Service?
It is shown by the Altar being raised as Mount Calvary was, and a cross placed upon it.

How else is it shown?
By the *Vestments* of the priest.
1. The *Amice* signifies the cloth Christ was blindfolded with.
2. The *Girdle*, the rope He was bound to the pillar by.
3. The *Alb*, the seamless robe.
4. The *Stole*, the yoke of our sins which He took on Him.
5. The *Maniple*, the handkerchief His face was wiped with.
6. The *Chasuble*, the scarlet robe the soldiers put on Him when they mocked Him.

How else is the Passion brought to mind?
By the *actions* of the priest.
1. He goes from point to point of the Altar to remind us how Christ was dragged before Annas, Caiaphas, and Pontius Pilate.
2. He washes his hands to call to mind the washing of the hands of Pontius Pilate.
3. After the Consecration he elevates the Sacrament as the Body of Christ was raised on the Cross.

1st SUNDAY AFTER EPIPHANY, Jan. 10th.

Have the other ceremonies in the Holy Eucharist any meaning?
Yes; they all set forth some great truth in action.
What do the lights mean?
That Christ is the True Light of the World.
What does the *unleavened* Bread mean?
That Christ is the Sinless Victim.
Why is water mixed with the wine?
Because from Christ's Side there flowed both Blood and Water.
Why is the Body of Christ laid upon the Corporal?
To remind us that Christ was wrapped in fine linen by St. Joseph of Arimathea.
Why is incense sometimes offered?
1. To signify the prayers of the Church.
2. To remind us that Holy Women brought spices for our Lord's Burial.

Why has Christ ordained these outward acts?
In order that our bodies and outward senses may worship Him as well as our souls.

AT ST. PETER'S, VAUXHALL.

Vicar: REV. E. DENNY.
Patrons: THE TRUSTEES.

THE following is a report of a High Celebration and of a Celebration "for the repose of the soul" of the late Vicar, at St. Peter's, Vauxhall:—

"Father" Herbert was one of the pioneers of the so-called "Catholic revival" in South London, and the remarkable work that he did at St. Peter's, Vauxhall, during the thirty years he was Vicar there was known and honoured far outside the limits of his parish. His character presented some curious contrasts. It was pointed out in the *Record* at the time of his death that, on the one hand, he was "a Ritualist of the Ritualists," and that, on the other, no Primitive Methodist could preach a simpler gospel than he preached. He died on November 14th, 1894, and he was succeeded in the living by the Rev. A. B. Sharpe. This gentleman, however, found the Ritualist position untenable in the Church of England, and in the summer of 1898 he 'verted to the Church of Rome. The present Vicar is evidently doing his best to maintain the advanced traditions of the Church, although the ritual at the High Celebration or Choral Communion, as I saw it, was much less elaborate than I expected. There were only two lights on the altar; no sacring-bell was rung, and there was no incense, although St. Peter's is one of the churches where, according to the *Tourist's Church Guide*, it is used on occasion. But the "appeal to the eye" in other respects was none the less effective; and one had no difficulty in determining by it the nature of the Eucharistic teaching prevalent at the church.

The celebrant was the junior curate. He wore the Eucharistic vestments, and was attended by two servers in tight-fitting garments, girdle, and white gauntlets. The bowings and the genuflections of this trio at and before the altar were very marked, while the prostrations of the servers during and after the consecration of the elements were most pronounced. The service, in its main outlines, followed the course with which readers of the *Record* will be familiar. One noteworthy interpolation in the service was the reading of the Collect for All Saints' Day in addition to the Collect for the Day.

The sermon was preached by the Vicar, who, however, before proceeding with it, made an important announcement. The next day would be the fourth anniversary of the death of George W. Herbert, and there would be at St. Peter's four celebrations of the Holy Eucharist "for the repose of his soul." I made a mental resolve that if it were possible I would attend one of these celebrations. But more of this presently. The Vicar, after eulogising the life-work of his predecessor, proceeded with his sermon, which was based on the Gospel for the Day. He had a great deal to say on lawlessness, and he stated the "Catholic" position. No doubt many might be puzzled, he said, when they heard priests, whom they had learned to reverence and love, branded as law-breakers. But they need not be alarmed; the position was this, that while the priests were ready to render a loyal obedience to Cæsar (the State) in regard to matters which came within the secular sphere, they declined to render unto Cæsar the things that were God's, and so they were called lawless. The Vicar admitted that he had put the matter crudely, but he was anxious to put it very simply. Crude and simple, indeed! It would surely have been more to the point if he had explained why many of the lawless clergy who have sworn to use the Prayer-book and no other yet take the Canon of the Mass as their guide when celebrating Holy Communion. It might also have had an interesting bearing on the question if the Vicar had explained to the congregation what is on those mysterious cards which stand on the altar at St. Peter's. But he was ominously silent on these questions.

The sermon over, the celebrant prepared the elements for consecration, washed the tips of his fingers, and proceeded with the service. He stood during the Confession, and made the sign of the cross when he pronounced the Absolution. The singing of the *Benedictus* was interpolated after the Prayer of Humble Access. The celebrant read the Prayer of Consecration in a low tone, and his voice when consecrating the wafer was quite inaudible. He elevated the wafer and the chalice, and the congregation bowed their heads. He genuflected before the elements himself, and his servers prostrated themselves during the whole time of the Prayer of Consecration. Immediately at the close of the prayer the hymn—

"Thee we adore, O hidden Saviour Thee,
 Who in Thy Sacrament dost deign to be,"

was sung, the people all kneeling meanwhile, and this was followed by the singing of the *Agnus*. There was only one communicant, even though there was a large congregation. The service shortly afterwards concluded. On leaving the church I noticed a large crucifix in relief on the north wall near the west door, and a space had been railed off in front

St. Peter's, Vauxhall

of it by forms. I concluded that this is the place where the clergy hear "confessions," in accordance with the notice exhibited at the west end of the church.

On the Monday morning the Holy Eucharist was celebrated four times "for the repose of the soul" of the late Mr. Herbert, who had been dead for four years. The hours of these celebrations were, I believe, 6.30 a.m., 7 a.m., 7.30 a.m., and 8 a.m. I got to the church as soon as the disorganised train traffic on a very foggy morning would allow. The services were held in a side-chapel where, curiously enough, the altar is placed against the west wall. The half-past seven celebration was in progress, the celebrant being the Vicar, vested in a black chasuble. The congregation was small, but no one communicated. Whether or not there were communicants at the two earlier services I am, of course, quite unable to say. At the eight o'clock celebration there was a larger congregation, four or five ladies attired as Sisters of Mercy being conspicuous amongst them. On or above the altar there were two candles burning, and there was also a small crucifix there. The celebrant, vested in a black chasuble, was the senior curate, and his junior colleague acted as server. The two paused together as they approached the steps of the altar and engaged in some private devotions. When this was over the celebrant went to the altar and began the service. It would be too wearisome to follow it in its intricate details; but it may be noted that the Collect, Epistle, and Gospel for the Day were quietly ignored. In their place the celebrant read the Collect from the Burial Office, "O Merciful God, the Father of our Lord Jesus Christ, Who is the resurrection and the life," &c.; a portion of 1 Cor. xv., "Now is Christ risen . . . every man in his own order," for the Epistle; and a passage from St. John for the Gospel. After the priest had prepared the Elements he washed his fingers and kissed the altar before proceeding with the service. During the Prayer of Consecration the curate server 'prostrated himself on the ground for some minutes in such a way as to suggest that he suffered considerable physical discomfort. The Prayer of Consecration was read in a soft voice—just audible; but the Manual Acts were hidden; the wafer and the chalice were elevated with great deliberation, and most of the congregation bowed themselves down in adoration. A few persons—some six or seven—communicated, but there was a larger number present at the service who did not do so.

On this report two questions at least arise:—

1. By whose authority was the Holy Eucharist celebrated four times before nine o'clock in one morning for "the repose of the soul" of the late Vicar? and
2. In what way did these services differ from Masses for the dead?

SOLEMN EUCHARIST AT ST. AGATHA'S, PORTSMOUTH.

Vicar: REV. G. H. TREMENHEERE.
Patrons: WINCHESTER COLLEGE.

THE new Church of St. Agatha, Portsmouth, has already made history. It is the headquarters of the Winchester College Mission, and was built under the direction of Father Dolling, whose missionary work amongst the soldiers, the sailors, and the poor of Portsmouth is well known throughout the country. Father Dolling's enterprise was conducted on the most advanced "Catholic" lines; every detail of it was known—or ought to have been known—to the Bishop of Winchester, but his lordship did not publicly interfere until the new church was ready for consecration. Then he came down and took exception to a third altar, which had been erected against the south wall of the church, because it was proposed to use it for the purpose of celebrations for the faithful departed. The controversy between the Bishop and the priest waxed strong; neither would give way, and ultimately Father Dolling resigned his charge. The Rev. G. H. Tremenheere was appointed in his stead, and, the cause of offence being taken away, the church was duly consecrated. I visited the church last Sunday, and to my astonishment I found that while the actual altar or table had been removed, the ledges above it, together with a large coloured crucifix in high relief, had been retained. There were flowers and candles on the ledges, and pinned against them were several memorial cards, while painted on some wooden panels on the wall, in gold letters, there is a long list of names (presumably of faithful departed). In the space in front there was a prayer-stool on which lay a stole ready for use, and I doubt not that it is here that the clergy of the church receive "confessions." But while the Bishop has refused to allow an altar against the south wall for celebrations for the faithful departed, he has not apparently forbidden these celebrations being performed elsewhere in the church, for just before the sermon on Sunday morning it was announced from the pulpit that this week "*the Holy Sacrifice will be offered for the faithful departed*" on Thursday. It is not easy, therefore, to determine the value of the Bishop's interference with Mr. Dolling in this matter. What loyal Churchmen object to is the service itself, and it makes but little difference to them whether it is performed in the south aisle, or in the side-chapel, or at the High Altar.

The church is built in the Italian style, and when it is finished will be a very handsome and costly building. The High Altar—on which, by-the-bye, there were six candles burning on Sunday—is, apparently, of a temporary character, for the original scheme provides for the erection of a baldachino and other accessories. The church is spacious, but I was surprised to see it so thinly attended on Sunday morning. For Morning Prayer, which was said very perfunctorily, there were not a score of persons present. The eleven o'clock service was styled Litany and solemn Eucharist, and this was much better attended; but, even so, I question whether the general congregation (apart from the school children) numbered more than 200. Moreover, as far as one could judge from their dress, they did not belong to the parish, which is an exceedingly poor one. The clergy-

St. Agatha's, Portsmouth 105

man who read the Litany (I think it was the Vicar) wore a green cope, and he had an acolyte kneeling on either side of him at the faldstool. The surpliced choir occupied seats in the west gallery. At the conclusion of the Litany the Vicar and his acolytes returned to the vestry, to reappear in a few minutes clad in the Eucharistic vestments. His chasuble was of light green with yellow trimmings, and was of a gaudy appearance. He was accompanied by two of the other clergy of the church more moderately attired in black cassocks and white cottas edged with lace; and he was attended by two servers, two acolytes, a censer-bearer and assistant, four of whom wore scarlet cassocks, white cottas edged with lace, and scarlet skull-caps. Some—perhaps all—of them had on scarlet felt slippers. Two carried lighted candles. The procession, as it wended its way from the vestry to the sacrarium, was a striking and effective display, and it was soon evident that the ritual of the service was to be of an advanced character. I propose, however, only to notice some of the principal points.

At the beginning of the service the priest censed the altar, and was in turn himself censed. He interpolated after the Collect for the Day the Collect for All Saints' Day. He read the Epistle at the south side, with his back to the people, and a hymn was afterwards interpolated while preparations were made for the ceremonial reading of the Gospel. The priest and his attendants left the altar and came down to the end of the sacrarium and grouped themselves on the north side. One of the servers supported the Gospel Book on his forehead, two others held lighted candles aloft, and two others brought in again the censer and incense. The priest made the sign of the cross on the Gospel Book, then censed it, and at the close of the reading kissed it. Incense was burning all the time that the Gospel was being read. The celebrant and his assistants returned to the altar for the Creed, and everyone knelt at the *Incarnatus*.

The sermon, by one of the curates, followed. It was a temperance discourse, but it was noteworthy for its assertion of priestism and its declaration that what the sinner needed for his restoration was repentance, confession, and the Sacraments. Sin could only be conquered, said the preacher, through the Sacraments.

During the offertory hymn the priest prepared the elements and afterwards washed his fingers. Incense was again freely used at this stage—altar, priest, curates, servers, and congregation being all censed in turn. The service proceeded. After the *Sursum Corda* some of the acolytes knelt in a row on a step below the priest, and just before the *Sanctus* they all doffed their skull-caps, and the candles were held aloft, while at the words "Holy, holy, holy" the sacring-bell was rung. The *Benedictus* was interpolated, and the Prayer of Consecration followed. It was fairly audible (I was sitting near the front), but the Manual Acts were completely hidden. The wafer and chalice were elevated, the bell was again rung three times, and the priest genuflected before the elements. During the Consecration Prayer the acolytes remained in the position above described, except that those in charge of the incense stood at the south side of the altar and manipulated the censer meanwhile. The singing of the *Agnus Dei* followed. At this stage a novelty was introduced. I have already alluded to the presence of the school children at the service. Sitting with them was a layman vested in cassock and surplice, and he directed their devotions. After the Prayer of Consecration he and they recited together some lines which, I think, are called "The Act of Worship." I regret I cannot give the exact words, but I have not the service-book in use at St. Agatha's. They seemed to be an acknowledgment of the presence of Christ on the altar through the act of the priest, and a prayer for a blessing upon the children, their parents, &c., and for mercy on the souls of the faithful departed. These words were a distinct interpolation in the service; they are not in the Prayer-book, or even conformable to the tenor of it. One of the servers received the Sacrament, but there were no communicants from the congregation, nor was any opportunity given for the purpose.

The service was shortly afterwards concluded. I doubt very much whether anything more "extreme" was ever practised in the church in Father Dolling's time, yet the Bishop of Winchester is one of the prelates who has endeavoured to minimise the perils of the present situation. But he was at the Lambeth Council, and may be about to act. If he will pay a visit to St. Agatha's he will find many things there that need his attention.

CHILDREN'S EUCHARIST AT ST. MICHAEL'S, PORTSMOUTH.

Vicar: REV. E. A. OMMANNEY.
Patron: THE BISHOP OF WINCHESTER.

ST. AGATHA'S is not the only "advanced" church in Portsmouth; St. Michael and All Angels' runs it very close. I have before me a paper which I brought away from the church on Sunday in which the seven Sacraments are taught, two as being "generally necessary for salvation" and "the other five" as "necessary for certain conditions of the Christian life." Moreover, "Sacraments need a validly ordained priest or bishop to celebrate them, for there can be no Sacraments apart from the Catholic Church." In the Parish Magazine, which I have also before me, "the Sacrament of Confession" is commended, and the Holy Communion is spoken of as the Mass. There is a "Children's Eucharist" every Sunday morning at 9.30, and on Sunday last when I attended the church there was a goodly number of children present. There is a Lady Chapel, but the Eucharist was celebrated at the High Altar. The priest wore the Eucharistic vestments, and was attended by two servers. Many of the children followed the service from a printed card, but the elder ones used Prayer-books. They do not seem now to use a children's service-book at St. Michael's, and at the celebration on Sunday the words of the Communion Office were fairly adhered to, except that

St. Michael's, Portsmouth

the Commandments were omitted and the Collect for All Saints' Day was added. But the service was to all intents and purposes a Mass. There was only one communicant. The *Benedictus* and the *Agnus* were sung. During the Prayer of Consecration (which was read in a very soft voice) the Manual Acts were hidden, the wafer and the chalice were elevated, the bell in the church tower was rung, and the priest genuflected before the elements. When the Bishop of Winchester goes to St. Agatha's he should also pay a visit to St. Michael's, for he will find there much that needs setting in order. We await with interest the results of the activity which the Bishops promise.

ANOTHER VISIT TO ST. ANSELM'S, STREATHAM.

THE account of a "celebration for the faithful departed" at St. Anselm's, Streatham, excited some attention at the time it was published, and there were not a few who thought that, inasmuch as the parish is not yet legally cut off, and as the Vicar-designate holds his position by virtue of the Bishop of Rochester's licence, at least some alteration in the conduct of the services would be demanded by the Bishop. It is also worthy of note that at the meeting of the Bishops in Council at Lambeth a course of action in regard to lawlessness was decided upon. Having these two facts in mind the correspondent of the *Record* again visited the church, wondering whether there would be any material alteration in the service, but there was none; the service was advertised in the Parish Magazine as "Celebration for the Faithful Departed," and it proceeded as before.

The celebrant was again the curate, the Rev. H. S. Milner, who does not hesitate to speak of this service as a Mass. He was vested, as before, in a chasuble of black silk with yellow trimmings, but this time he was attended by a server, while on the previous occasion he was alone. The service was held in the Lady Chapel, and the congregation was exceedingly small—three or four. There were two candles burning on the retable. Before beginning the service the celebrant stood at the steps of the altar and evidently engaged in some private devotions. Whether or not they were in any way connected with the Roman Missal it is impossible to say; but the attitude of the priest and his server was significant. I also gravely doubt whether he used the Book of Common Prayer, "and none other," for the service. The point is one of such extreme importance that I invite him to produce to the Editor of the *Record*, for independent examination, the book from which he conducted this service. He omitted the Commandments, but for what reason I cannot say. Certainly not to save time, for a great deal more time was spent in intervals during the service (while the priest was engaged in ceremonies and devotions at the altar) than would be taken up in reciting the Commandments in accordance with the rubric. He read a strange Collect, Epistle, and Gospel. I cannot give the references, for he read them so quickly, and in such a low voice, that I could only catch a word here and there. I believe that the Collect from the Burial Office, " Almighty God, with Whom do live," &c., was used; that the Epistle was taken from 1 Thessalonians; and that the Gospel was from St. John vi. These, it will be seen, were not according to the order for the day.

After the offertory there was a long pause, during which the priest seemed to use privately some prayers from the service-book, and finally he read the Prayer for the Church Militant, pausing slightly after certain words. I observe that in the "Ordinary of the Mass" there is a rubric directing this to be done. There was also a pause before the Prayer of Consecration, during which the priest was reading from his service-book and making the sign of the cross over the elements. Here, again, it is significant that the "Canon of the Mass" provides certain prayers for use by the priest at this stage. It also directs the priest to "kiss the altar." Mr. Milner kissed the altar. The Prayer of Consecration was read in a low voice, and the Manual Acts were completely hidden, for Mr. Milner bowed his head over the altar. At the words of consecration the server rang the sacring-bell, and the bell in the church tower was tolled (as it had been at the *Sanctus*). The celebrant genuflected before the elements, and afterwards elevated the Host and the chalice. There are no rubrical directions for all this in the Book of Common Prayer, but the "Canon of the Mass" tells the priest when to bow his head over the altar, when to genuflect and worship, and when to elevate the Host and the chalice. At the close of the prayer the priest, still standing with his back to the people, extended his arms right and left for a moment or two, then brought them down again, and several times made the sign of the cross over the elements. He seemed to be engaged in some ceremony, and he obviously took his directions from his service-book. These proceedings lasted for some minutes, and afterwards the priest communicated himself, the sacring-bell being again rung and the bell in the tower tolled. Afterwards he turned to the people and, holding the chalice in his left hand and the wafer in his right above it, made the sign of the cross with the wafer, uttered some words which sounded like "The Body of our Lord Jesus Christ which was given for thee," and then immediately turned back again without waiting to see whether anyone desired to communicate; and, as a matter of fact, there were no communicants, neither were there any when I attended the service previously. He then read the Lord's Prayer and the Collect following. The *Gloria in Excelsis* and the Blessing were omitted. But the priest remained at the altar for some little time, performing the ablutions and saying privately more prayers from his service-book. This service-book, I conjecture, was not the Book of Common Prayer; and I again invite Mr. Milner to produce it for inspection.

THE ROMAN MISSAL IN ENGLISH CHURCHES.

THE occasional attendant at such "lawless" services as have been described over and over again in the columns of the *Record* frequently discovers that he cannot follow all that is going on. It is plain to him that the celebrant priest and his helpers are engaged in devotions other than those of the Prayer-book. Sometimes these devotions are—shall we say?—obscured by a hymn, or the *Agnus Dei*, being sung by the choir. But in any case the hearer is conscious that an elaborate service is proceeding amongst the clergy and their helpers to which the Book of Common Prayer offers no clue. It is no case of a few private prayers silently said by one man, but of devotions evidently complicated and shared alike by the celebrant and his helpers; of devotions which palpably follow some familiar and elaborate rite in which parts of our own Communion Service seem afterwards to have been incorporated. The extreme, some might say indecent, haste with which these devotions are conducted might blind the careless observer to their length and importance. But no one can ignore the general divergence at once suggested from the Order found in the Prayer-book.

What are these other devotions? Whence do they come?

To such as may not know the answer to these questions I am able to offer a simple explanation, so simple in its revelation of disloyalty to our Church that those who are unprepared may find it hard to credit the facts. These can, however, be verified by all who care to do so.

I have before me a little book, entitled *The Server's Guide at a Low Celebration of the Holy Eucharist*, by "the Editors of the *Order of Divine Service*," &c. (Third Edition. Mowbray and Co.). In this, after "a few plain rules for the server," I come upon full directions for the duty of the server in a "Low Celebration." It is hardly necessary to do more than call attention to the "Preparatory Prayer which may be said before vesting," save to point out that the server is made to say, "O Almighty Lord of heaven and earth, behold I presume to appear before Thee this day, to assist in offering to Thee . . . Thy Son." Our main interest, however, is with the "Order at a Low Celebration of the Holy Eucharist," which follows. In this book, though distinctions of type are carefully made, and directions profusely offered, there is not a word, not a syllable, to show that any part of the "Order" is foreign to the Book of Common Prayer.

Let us see how this order opens. We quote the directions to the server with the text of the service :—

THE ORDER
AT A
LOW CELEBRATION OF THE HOLY EUCHARIST.

Arrived at the steps of the Altar, receive the Priest's Biretta, and with him make proper reverence to the Altar. Put down Biretta, place Missal (closed) on its stand, and then kneel on floor at the opposite side of the Altar.

The Priest, standing at the foot of the Altar, signs himself with the sign of the Cross, and says :—

✠ In the Name of the FATHER, and of the SON, and of the HOLY GHOST. Amen.

Then, joining his hands before his breast, he says :—

I will go unto the Altar of GOD.

Server.—Even unto the GOD of my joy and gladness.

Psalm xliii. Judica.

Priest.—Give sentence with me, O GOD, and defend my cause against the ungodly people: O deliver me from the deceitful and wicked man.

Server.—For Thou art the GOD of my strength, why hast Thou put me from Thee, and why go I so heavily when the enemy oppresseth me?

Priest.—O send out Thy light and Thy truth that they may lead me, and bring me unto Thy holy hill, and to Thy dwelling.

Server.—And that I may go unto the Altar of GOD, even unto the GOD of my joy and gladness, and upon the harp will I give thanks unto Thee, O GOD, my GOD.

P.—Why art thou so heavy, O my soul, and why art thou so disquieted within me?

S.—O put thy trust in GOD, for I will yet give Him thanks which is the help of my countenance and my God.

P.—Glory be to the FATHER, and to the SON, and to the HOLY GHOST.

S.—As it was in the beginning, is now, and ever shall be, world without end. Amen.

P.—I will go unto the Altar of GOD.

S.—Even unto the GOD of my joy and gladness.

P.—✠ Our help is in the Name of the LORD.

S.—Who hath made Heaven and earth.

The Priest, bowing down, says the Confession:—

I confess to Almighty GOD . . . for me.

S.—May Almighty GOD have mercy upon thee, forgive thee thy sins and bring thee to everlasting life.

P.—Amen.

S.—I confess to Almighty GOD, to blessed Mary ever Virgin, to blessed Michael the Archangel, to blessed John Baptist, to the holy Apostles Peter and Paul, to all the Saints, and to you, father, that I have sinned exceedingly in thought, word, and deed, through my fault, through my fault, through my most grievous fault. Therefore I beg blessed Mary ever Virgin, blessed Michael the Archangel, blessed John Baptist, the holy Apostles Peter and Paul, all the Saints, and you, father, to pray to the LORD our GOD for me.

Then the Priest gives the Absolution, saying:—

May Almighty God have mercy . . . everlasting life.
S.—Amen.
P.—✠ May the Almighty and Merciful LORD grant us pardon, absolution, and remission of our sins.
S.—Amen.
P.—Wilt Thou not turn again, and quicken us, O LORD?
S.—That Thy people may rejoice in Thee.
P.—Show us Thy mercy, O LORD.
S.—And grant us Thy salvation.
P.—O LORD, hear my prayer.
S.—And let my cry come unto Thee.
P.—The LORD be with you.
S.—And with thy spirit.
P.—Let us pray.

When the Priest ascends to the Altar, go and kneel on the lowest step on the opposite side to the Missal. As he ascends to the Altar, the Priest says:—

We beseech Thee, O LORD, to take away from us our iniquities: that we may be worthy to enter with pure minds into the Holy of holies. Through CHRIST our LORD. Amen.

Bowing down and kissing the Altar, he says:—

We beseech Thee, O LORD, by the merits of all Thy saints, that Thou wouldst vouchsafe to forgive me all my sins. Amen.

Having read the Introit, he says:—

Our FATHER, &c.

Here, then, we have an Order which is in every detail alien from that in the Prayer-book. As already said, we come quite suddenly upon the beginning of the Prayer-book service without any intimation that the preceding matter has been foisted in. Actually, however, the celebrant and his server conduct these devotions in such a way that the congregation hear little of them, although conscious that they are going on. I pass over much that is extraneous

The Roman Missal in English Churches 117

until we reach the end of the offertory sentences. Then the "Order" proceeds :—

After the Priest has made the Oblations, bring the Water Cruet with the dish and napkin, and standing below the predella, assist at the washing of the Priest's fingers. Having replaced the Cruet, &c., on the Credence, return and kneel at your usual place.

[*P.*—Brethren, pray that this my Sacrifice and yours may be acceptable to GOD the FATHER Almighty.

S.—The LORD receive the Sacrifice at thy hands, to the praise and glory of His Name, to our benefit and that of all His Holy Church.

P.—Amen.

Here follow the Secrets, at the end of the last the Priest says :
World without end.

S.—Amen.]

What is the source of this passage and of the Devotions to which it refers? On p. 14, again, we have this :—

[*In the Prayers following the Consecration, when the Priest says, in a somewhat louder tone,* To us also Thy sinful servants, *bow your head and strike your breast once.*
When you hear the Priest say world without end, *respond* Amen.
The Priest then says Let us pray *and the Lord's Prayer down to* And lead us not into temptation.]

What are these "Prayers following the Consecration"? But to proceed: according to this "Order" the service does not end with the Blessing; there is much more, part of which is set out as follows :—

After the Priest has taken the Ablutions and covered the Chalice, he reads the Communion, and says :—

[The LORD be with you.
S.—And with thy spirit.]

He then reads the Post Communions; at the end of the first and last, respond [Amen].

When the Priest has concluded the Post Communions and goes to

the centre, pass to the Epistle side, and if he has not closed the Book remove it at once to the Gospel corner.
During the Last Gospel stand, as usual, at the Epistle side.
[*P.*—The LORD be with you.
S.—And with thy spirit.]
When the Priest announces the Gospel make the three signs of the Cross ✠ ✠ ✠ as usual, and respond:—
[Glory be to Thee, O Lord.]
Genuflect if the Priest does so and at the same time, and say, at the conclusion of the Gospel [Thanks be to God.]

Now, with all allowance for what may fairly be called private devotions, it is clear that the service here presented is so total a corruption of that in the Book of Common Prayer as to be wholly unlike it. It is not the old use of Sarum. What is it? I shall presently explain.

Some of the omissions from this little volume may be filled up from one entitled *Aids to Reverently Celebrating the Holy Eucharist* (Griffith, Farran, and Co. Third Edition). I pass over much that is interesting to deal with these private devotions. There is a "Preparation for Mass," which is "to be said according to the opportunity of the priest," and a "Thanksgiving after Mass." There is an interesting footnote to the latter intimating that "A translation of the additional prayers and thanksgivings *from the Breviary* will be found in the 'Day Office' (Masters)." Then comes a section headed "The Priest's Secret Prayers at Mass," to which title this footnote is appended:—

This title is frequently given to the prayers at Mass which the priest does not say audibly: they can scarcely be called "private prayers." The "*secreta*" or "*secret*" is quite distinct from them, and consists of some prayers directed in the Missal to be said after the offertory and before the preface.

So, then, the "Secreta" of the other book "can scarcely be called 'private prayers.'" The admission is worth

The Roman Missal in English Churches 119

remembering. "The Preparation said with the Server at the Altar" is nearly identical with the opening passages of the *Server's Guide*, pointing to the common origin. Then come "Secret Prayers during the Office," with this significant intimation by way of preface :—

> *Owing to the varying opinions held by priests as to the portions of the secret prayers they wish to use or omit, a translation in full is given from the Roman Missal, omitting only some of the ritual directions respecting the paten, which seem inconsistent with its being used as a receptacle for the people's Hosts.*

The source thus frankly indicated, we need not, perhaps, go at length into what follows. A single extract will serve to show the kind of devotions put into the mouths of English clergy :—

COMMEMORATION OF THE LIVING.

Remember, O Lord, Thy servants and handmaidens *M.* and *N.* [*he joins his hands, and prays for those he intends to pray for; then extending them*] and all here present whose faith is known to Thee, and whose devotion Thou beholdest; for whom we offer, or who are themselves offering unto Thee this sacrifice of praise for themselves and for all that belong to them, for the redemption of their souls, for the hope of their salvation and safety; and who pay their vows to Thee, the eternal, living, and true God.

Joining in communion with, and reverencing in the first place the memory of the glorious and ever Virgin Mary, Mother of our God and Lord Jesus Christ; as also of Thy blessed apostles and martyrs Peter and Paul, Andrew, James, John, Thomas, James, Philip, Bartholomew, Matthew, Simon and Thaddeus, Linus, Cletus, Clement, Sixtus, Cornelius, Cyprian, Laurence, Chrysogonus, John and Paul, Cosmas and Damian, and of all Thy saints; to whose merits and prayers do Thou grant that we may in all things be defended by the help of Thy protection [*he joins his hands*] : through the same Christ our Lord. Amen.

I shall presently show the source of this. There is much more which it might be useful to quote, but I forbear.

I end by asking, What service is it?

To answer the question I turn to the Roman Catholic Missal,

and follow the service used to-day by the Roman Church. I find that "Ordinary of the Mass" begins as follows:—

In nomine Patris, ✠ et Filii, et Spiritus Sancti. Amen.
Introibo ad altare Dei.
R. Ad Deum, qui lætificat juventutem meam.
S. Judica me, Deus, et discerne causam meam de gente non sancta : ab homine iniquo et doloso erue me.
M. Quia tu es, Deus, fortitudo mea, quare me repulisti ? et quare tristis incedo dum affligit me inimicus ?
S. Emitte lucem tuam et veritatem tuam : ipso me deduxerunt et adduxerunt in montem sanctum tuum, et in tabernacula tua.
M. Et introibo ad altare Dei : ad Deum, qui lætificat juventutem meam.
S. Confitebor tibi in cithara, Deus, Deus meus : quare tristis es, anima mea ? et quare conturbas me ?
M. Spera in Deo, quoniam adhuc confitebor illi : salutare vultus mei, et Deus meus.
S. Gloria Patri, et Filio, et Spiritui Sancto.
M. Sicut erat in principio, et nunc, et semper, et in sæcula sæculorum. Amen.
V. Introibo ad altare Dei.
R. Ad Deum, qui lætificat juventutem meam.
V. Adjutorium nostrum in nomine Domini.
R. Qui fecit cœlum et terram.
S. Confiteor Deo omnipotenti, etc.
M. Misereatur tui omnipotens Deus, et dimissis peccatis tuis, perducat te ad vitam æternam.
S. Amen.
M. Confiteo Deo omnipotenti, beatæ Mariæ semper Virgini, beato Michaeli Archangelo, beato Joanni Baptistæ, sanctis Apostolis Petro et Paulo, omnibus Sanctis, et tibi pater, quia peccavi nimis cogitatione, verbo, et opere, mea culpa, mea culpa, mea maxima culpa. Ideo precor beatam Mariam semper Virginem, beatum Michaelem Archangelum, beatum Joannem Baptistam, sanctos Apostolos Petrum et Paulum, omnes Sanctos, et te pater, orare pro me ad Dominum Deum nostrum.
S. Misereatur vestri omnipotens Deus, et dimissis peccatis vestris, perducat vos ad vitam æternam.
M. Amen.

The Roman Missal in English Churches

S. ✠ Indulgentiam, absolutionem, et remissionem peccatorum nostrorum tribuat nobis omnipotens et misericors Dominus.
M. Amen.
V. Deus, tu conversus vivificabis nos.
R. Et plebs tua lætabitur in te.
V. Ostende nobis, Domine, misericordiam tuam.
R. Et salutare tuum da nobis.
V. Domine, exaudi orationem meam.
R. Et clamor meus ad te veniat.
V. Dominus vobiscum.
R. Et cum spiritu tuo.

Aufer a nobis, quæsumus, Domine, iniquitates nostras; ut ad Sancta sanctorum puris mereamur mentibus introire. Per Christum Dominum nostrum. Amen.

Oramus te, Domine, per merita sanctorum tuorum quorum reliquiæ hic sunt, et omnium sanctorum, ut indulgere digneris omnia peccata mea. Amen.

So, then, we are using, not the English Prayer-book, but the Roman Mass-book, save that we are offered an English translation. I pass on to consider my second quotation from the *Server's Guide*. Here is the corresponding quotation from the same Roman source :—

Orate, fratres, ut meum ac vestrum sacrificium acceptabile fiat apud Deum Patrem omnipotentem.

R. Suscipiat Dominus sacrificium de manibus tuis, ad laudem et gloriam nominis sui, ad utilitatem quoque nostram, totiusque Ecclesiæ suæ sanctæ.

"The Secrets" follow in both cases.

The third quotation is readily explained by reference to the Roman Canon of the Mass. As "the Prayers following the Consecration" are not set out, I cannot prove their identity; but in the Canon of the Mass after the appointed adoration of the Host, adoration of the chalice, and prayers for the dead, the priest is instructed to *raise his voice* and proceed, "*Nobis quoque peccatoribus famulis tuis,*" &c. Later on is the direction to the priest to say aloud, "*Per omnia sæcula sæculorum.*" The final quotation from the same book in like manner follows the Missal.

The secret prayers quoted from the *Aids to Reverently Celebrating* are taken bodily from the Roman Canon of the Mass.

In fine, what we have here is the Mass according to the modern Roman Use—followed in the Roman churches in England to-day—into which bits of the Communion Service have been dovetailed. It is an English Church. The clergy are English clergy. They have, at one of the most solemn moments of their lives, made this oath :—

I assent to the Thirty-nine Articles of Religion, and to the Book of Common Prayer, and of the Ordering of Bishops, Priests, and Deacons. I believe the doctrine of the Church of England, as therein set forth, to be agreeable to the Word of God : and *in Public Prayer and Administration of the Sacraments I will use the Form in the said Book prescribed, and none other, except so far as shall be ordered by lawful authority.*

And this is how they keep it.

———

"That it may please Thee to bring into the way of truth all such as have erred and are deceived.

"*We beseech Thee to hear us, good Lord.*"

THE ROMAN MASS-BOOK IN ENGLISH CHURCHES:

THE MISSAL AND THE PRAYER-BOOK COMBINED.

THE foregoing pages have made it evident that the Roman Missal furnishes the office-book by which much of the service of Holy Communion is conducted in some extreme English churches. I shall now enable English Churchpeople again to judge of the extent to which lawless clergy permit themselves to ignore their own Prayer-book by setting side by side the Roman Missal and an instruction for celebrating Mass in English churches, from a book entitled *Ceremonial of the Altar*, "Compiled by a Priest" (Sonnenschein and Co.) It will be seen that the corresponding parts do not always come in the same order :—

CEREMONIAL OF THE ALTAR.	THE MISSAL.
ORDINARY OF THE MASS.	ORDINARY OF THE MASS.
Whilst the Priest is putting on the sacred vestments, let him say this hymn:	
"Come, Holy Ghost. . . ."	
	In nomine Patris . . .
Then let him say:—	
I will go unto the Altar of God.	Introibo ad altare Dei . . .
Psalm xliii.	Psalm xliii.
"Give sentence . . ."	Judica me . . .
Glory be . . .	Gloria Patri . . .

CEREMONIAL OF THE ALTAR.	THE MISSAL.
I will go unto the Altar of God.	Introibo ad altare . . . Ad Deum, qui . . . Adjutorium nostrum . . . Qui fecit . . .
Lord, have mercy. Christ „ „ Lord „ „ Our Father . . . Hail Mary, full of grace . . . Hail Mary, mother of God . . .	
Then standing at the step of the altar, and humbly bowing down, let him say:— And lead us not into temptation; But deliver us from evil. Confess unto the Lord, for He is gracious, And His mercy endureth for ever.	
I confess to God, to Blessed Mary . . . Almighty God have mercy upon you . . .	Confiteor Deo Omnipotenti . . . Misereatur tui . . .
After this the Ministers say:— I confess . . .	Confiteor Deo Omnipotenti, Beatæ Mariæ . . .
And the Priest answers:— Almighty God, *as above.*	Misereatur vestri, Omnipotens Deus . . .
Then let the Priest add:— The Almighty and Merciful God grant you absolution . . .	S. Indulgentiam, absolutionem, et remissionem peccatorum nostrorum tribuat nobis omnipotens et misericors Dominus.
Our help standeth . . . Who hath made . . .	V. Deus, tu conversus vivificabis nos.

The Roman Mass-book in English Churches 125

CEREMONIAL OF THE ALTAR.	THE MISSAL.
Blessed be the name . . . From this time forth.	R. Et plebs tua lætabitur in te. V. Ostende nobis, Domine, misericordiam tuam. R. Et salutare tuum da nobis. V. Domine, exaudi orationem meam. R. Et clamor meus ad te veniat. V. Dominus vobiscum. R. Et cum spiritu tuo.
Then ascending to the altar . . . he says silently:— "Take away from us, we beseech Thee, O Lord, all our iniquities," &c.	*Ascending to the altar, he says secretly:—* Aufer a nobis quæsumus, Domine, iniquitates nostras, &c.
Passing to the right side of the altar, he reads the Introit for the day . . .	*The Priest, signing himself with the sign of the Cross, reads the Introit.*
[The Lord's Prayer, the Collect for Purity, and the Commandments follow.]	[The Kyrie Eleison and the Gloria in Excelsis follow.]
"The Lord be with you." "And with thy spirit."	Dominus vobiscum. Et cum spiritu tuo.
[The Prayer for the Queen, the Collects, and the Epistle follow.]	[The Collects from the Missal and the Epistle follow.]
Then he reads the Gradual, &c.	*Then the Gradual, Tract, Alleluia, or Sequence.*
". . . The Lord be in my heart and in my mouth," &c. "The Lord be with you." "And with thy spirit."	Dominus sit in corde meo et in labiis meis, &c. Dominus vobiscum. Et cum spiritu tuo.
[The reading of the Gospel and of the Nicene Creed follow.]	[The reading of the Gospel and of the Nicene Creed follow.]
"The Lord be with you," &c.	Dominus vobiscum, &c.

CEREMONIAL OF THE ALTAR.	THE MISSAL.
Then is said the offertory. After the Priest has said this . . . he receives the Bread and Wine and water from the server.	*Then he reads the offertory, and taking the Paten with the Host, says:—*
Before he adds the water, he says:—	"Suscipe, sancte Pater," &c.
"May it be blessed by the Lord, from Whose side," &c.	*Pouring water and wine into the Chalice, he says:—*
	"Deus, qui humanæ substantiæ dignitatem mirabiliter condidisti et mirabilius reformasti," &c.
As he offers the Chalice and Paten, he says:—	*Offering up the Chalice, he says:—*
"Receive, O Holy Trinity, this oblation, which I, an unworthy sinner, offer to Thine honour, and in reverence of Blessed Mary and of all Thy saints, for my sins and offences; for the salvation of the living and the repose of all the holy dead. In the Name of the Father, and of the Son, and of the Holy Ghost, may this new sacrifice be acceptable to Almighty God."	"Offerimus tibi, Domine, calicem salutaris," &c.
	Bowing down, he says:—
	". . . et sic fiat sacrificium nostrum in conspectu tuo hodie, ut placeat tibi, Domine Deus."
Then going to the Epistle side, he washes his fingers, saying:—	*Washing his fingers, he recites the following:—*
"Cleanse me, O Lord, from all defilement of mind and body that so I may perform the holy work of the Lord."	"Lavabo inter innocentes manus meas; et circumdabo altare tuum Domine," &c.
Returning to the midst of the altar, and bowing down with joined hands, he says:—	*Bowing before the altar, he says:—*
"In a spirit of humility and contrition may we be accepted of Thee, O Lord," &c.	"Suscipe, sancta Trinitas, hanc oblationem quam tibi offerimus," &c.

The Roman Mass-book in English Churches 127

CEREMONIAL OF THE ALTAR.	THE MISSAL.
Turning to the people, he says:— "Brethren and sisters, pray for me that this our common sacrifice may be accepted by the Lord our God."	*Turning to the people, he says:—* "Orate, frates, ut meum ac vestrum sacrificium acceptabile fiat apud Deum Patrem omnipotentem.
Turning again to the altar, he recites, with hands extended, the Secret Prayers, saying aloud at the end, "World without end."	*He then recites the Secret Prayers, which being finished he says in an audible voice:—* "Per omnia sæcula sæculorum."
[The Prayer for the Church Militant, the Invitation, the Confession, the Absolution, the Comfortable Words, the *Sursum Corda*, the Preface, and the *Sanctus* follow.]	[The *Sursum Corda*, the Preface, and the *Sanctus* follow.]
"Blessed is He that cometh in the Name of the Lord. Hosanna in the Highest."	"Benedictus qui venit in nomine Domini. Hosanna in excelsis."
[The Prayer of Humble Access follows.]	
THE CANON OF THE MASS.	THE CANON OF THE MASS.

[The prayers which follow are too long for quotation in full. We give the opening sentences from the "*Ceremonial*" and the "*Missal*" respectively. They are practically identical throughout.]

"Thee, therefore, O most merciful Father, through Jesus Christ, Thy Son, our Lord, we humbly pray and beseech [*he raises himself after kissing the altar*] that Thou would accept and bless these gifts, these offerings, this holy and unspotted sacrifice," &c.	"Te igitur, clementissime Pater, per Jesum Christum Filium tuum Dominum nostrum [he kisses the altar] supplices rogamus ac petimus uti accepta habeas et benedicas hæc dona," &c.

THE CANON OF THE MASS.

"Remember, O Lord, Thy servants," &c.

"Joining in communion with, and reverently commemorating first the glorious and ever Virgin [*he inclines a little*] Mary, Mother of our God and Lord Jesus Christ," &c.

He lays his hands on the altar, on each side of the Corporal, and, regarding the Host with reverence, proceeds:—

"This oblation, therefore, of our service, as also of Thy whole family [*he raises his hands and his eyes*], we beseech Thee, O Lord, graciously to accept," &c.

"Which oblation do Thou, O God, vouchsafe in all respects to make blessed, approved, ratified, reasonable, and acceptable, that it may become to us the Body and the Blood of Thy most dearly beloved Son Jesus Christ."

[The Prayer of Consecration follows. After the words of Consecration, the direction is]

Having adored, he elevates the Host above his head, saying:—

"Do this in remembrance of Me."

Then reverently replacing the Host he again adores.

"Likewise after Supper . . . Remission of Sins." *After adoring he elevates the chalice, saying:* "Do this . . . in remembrance of Me."

THE CANON OF THE MASS.

"Memento, Domine, famulorum," &c.

"Communicantes, et memoriam venerantes, imprimis gloriosæ semper Virginis Mariæ, Genitricis Dei et Domini nostri Jesu Christi," &c.

Spreading his hands over the oblation, he says:—

"Hanc igitur oblationem servitutis nostræ, sed et cunctæ familiæ tuæ quæsumus, Domine ut placatus accipias," &c.

"Quam oblationem, tu Deus, in omnibus quæsumus benedictam, adscriptam, ratam, rationabilem acceptabilemque facere digneris; ut nobis corpus et sanguis fiat dilectissimi Filii tui Domini nostri Jesu Christi."

After pronouncing the words of Consecration the Priest, kneeling, adores the Sacred Host, and, rising, he elevates it.

"Simili modo . . . in mei memoriam facietis."

Kneeling, he adores, and, rising, elevates the chalice.

The Roman Mass-book in English Churches

THE CANON OF THE MASS.

He replaces the chalice, covers it, and again adores. Stretching out his arms in the form of a cross, he proceeds:

"Wherefore, O Lord, we, Thy servants and holy people, mindful of the blessed passion of the same Thy Son, our Lord Jesus Christ, His Resurrection from the dead, and His glorious ascension into heaven," &c.

Here he crosses his arms upon his breast and, inclining his body, says:—

"We humbly beseech Thee, Almighty God, command these gifts," &c.

He joins his hands and prays for such of the dead as he desires.

"To them, O Lord," &c.

He strikes his breast once, saying:—

"To us, also, Thy sinful servants," &c.

"Deliver us, O Lord, we beseech Thee, from all evils ... [*he takes the Paten, kisses it, places it before his left and then his right eye, after which he makes the sign of the Cross with it upon himself, and then replaces it on the altar, saying*] graciously give peace in our time," &c.

"O Lamb of God," &c.

"May this most holy union of the Body and Blood," &c.

THE CANON OF THE MASS.

"Unde et memores Domine, nos servi tui, sed et plebs tua sancta, ejusdem Christi Filii tui Domini nostri tam beatæ passionis necnon et ab inferis resurrectionis, sed et in cælos gloriosæ ascensionis," &c.

Bowing down, he says:—

"Supplices te rogamus omnipotens Deus, jube, hæc," &c.

He prays for such of the dead as he intends to pray for.

"Ipsis, Domine," &c.

Here, striking his breast and slightly raising his voice, he says:—

"Nobis quoque peccatoribus," &c.

"Libera nos, quæsumus, Domine, ab omnibus malis ... [*making the sign of the Cross on himself with the Paten, he kisses it, and says*] da propitius pacem in diebus nostris," &c.

"Hæc commixtio et consecratio corporis et sanguinis," &c.

"Agnus Dei," &c.

K

THE CANON OF THE MASS.

He says privately the following Prayers before his own communion:—

"O Lord Jesus Christ, Son of the living God," &c.

"Let not the Sacrament of Thy Body and Blood, O Lord Jesus Christ, which I, albeit unworthy, receive, be to me for judgment and condemnation," &c.

Again inclining towards the Host, he says:—

"Hail evermore, Most Holy Flesh of Christ. . . May the Body of our Lord Jesus Christ be to me, a sinner, the Way and the Life."

Here he receives the Body, making a cross with the same before his mouth. Then to the Blood he says with great devotion:—

"Hail for evermore. . . May the Body and Blood of our Lord Jesus Christ avail to me a sinner as an eternal healing unto life everlasting. . . ."

Here he receives the Blood, which taken, and the chalice again covered, he adores, and says with devotion the prayer following before he communicates the people:—

"I give thanks unto Thee, O Lord, Holy Father," &c.

THE CANON OF THE MASS.

"Domine Jesu Christe, Fili Dei vivi," &c.

"Perceptio corporis tui, Domine Jesu Christe, quod ego indignus sumere præsumo, non mihi proveniat in judicium et condemnationem," &c.

Making a genuflection, the Priest rises and says:—

"Panem cœlestem accipiam . . . Domine, non sum dignus . . . Corpus Domini nostri Jesu Christi custodiat animam meam in vitam æternam."

He then receives the Sacred Host, and after a short pause says:—

"Quid retribuam Domino pro omnibus quæ retribuit mihi?"

Receiving the chalice, he says:—

"Sanguis Domini nostri Jesu Christi," &c.

The Roman Mass-book in English Churches 131

THE CANON OF THE MASS.

Turning by his right, and descending the steps of the altar to the communicants, if there be any, he administers the Holy Communion, saying to each
[The Prayer-book words.]

Then returning to the altar he covers the chalice with the pall, adores, and, extending his hands, says aloud, the people repeating after him every petition:—

"Our Father," &c.
"The Lord be with you."
"And with Thy Spirit."
"O Lord and Heavenly Father," &c.

Then he reads the Post-Communion for the day.

Then shall be said or sung:—

"Glory be to God on high," &c.
"The peace of God," &c.
[After consuming what remains of the Sacrament.]

Then he takes the first ablution, of wine, saying:—

"Grant, O Lord, that what we have received with our mouth we may retain with a pure mind," &c.

Then the second, of wine and water, poured over his fingers, saying:—

THE CANON OF THE MASS.

Then the Priest, turning to the communicants . . . administers the Holy Communion, saying to each
[The form and act of communicating the people are, of course, different in the Roman Church.]

Taking the first ablution, he says:—

"Quod ore sumpsimus, Domine, pura mente capiamus," &c.

Taking the second ablution, he says:—

THE CANON OF THE MASS.	THE CANON OF THE MASS.
"May this Communion, O Lord, cleanse us from sin, and make us partakers of the heavenly healing."	"Corpus tuum Domine, quod sumpsi, et sanguis quem potavi, adhæreat visceribus meis," &c.
Then he bows and says:— "Let us venerate the sign of the Cross," &c.	
Then he folds up the Corporal and places it in the Burse, and having veiled the vessels in the usual way he bows his body and says, with joined hands:— "O most Holy Trinity, grant that this my bounden duty and service may be pleasing unto Thee," &c.	*He then wipes the chalice, which he covers; and having folded the Corporal places it on the altar; he then reads the Communion. . . . Then he reads the Post-Communion. . . . Bowing down before the Altar he says:—* "Placeat tibi, sancta Trinitas, obsequium servitutis meæ," &c.
In returning to the sacristy he recites the first fourteen verses of the Gospel according to St. John.	*He then begins the Gospel according to St. John.*

The identity of these two service-books is practically complete, and, in the light of the comparison instituted above, Churchmen will now the better understand whence the celebrant obtains his instructions for those strange doings which have been referred to in the *Record* accounts (here reprinted) of High Celebrations, &c., in various churches. It will also enable them to understand what the priest is doing and saying (often inaudibly) during the long pauses which have been frequently noted by our correspondents. The "use" varies in different churches—more often than not, we expect, according to the whim or caprice of the individual priest; but no one can attend a High Celebration at an "advanced" church without being conscious that the celebrant is taking some

The Roman Mass-book in English Churches 133

other book than the Book of Common Prayer for his guide. We affirm that he uses the Ordinary and the Canon of the Mass adapted from the Roman Missal for English use. Yet he has made a distinct promise at the most solemn moment of his life that he will use in his public ministrations the Prayer-book " and none other."

The object of the compiler of such books as *The Ceremonial of the Altar* is frankly stated by the author of that manual :—

"The result aimed at has been to put the student in possession of the traditions of the method of saying Mass which the compilers of our Prayer-book presupposed to exist, and which, though some stray fragments of them have lasted on to our own time, gradually died out in the course of the evil times that the Church of England has had to pass through since the sixteenth century."

But the writer is conscious that there may be objectors even amongst those of his own party to the use of this book, and he accordingly offers explanations. To those who recoil from the personal trouble of becoming familiar with so many rules and directions he replies in the words of the familiar text, " I will not offer unto the Lord my God of that which doth cost me nothing." To those whose objection has reference not to themselves, but to their people, he says that "the pious extravagances of a High Churchman are far more likely to offend than the reverent and subdued action of a Catholic." To a third class of objectors, who think that the time required to say so many additional prayers would be so great that the people would be wearied, he replies as follows :—

"This, however, is a complete fallacy; for it is a matter of everyday experience that it is precisely those priests who say their Mass most carefully and well who occupy the least time in doing it. Many of the prayers are appointed to be said while some necessary action is performed, so that no time is lost by saying them. Besides this, the time that is wasted by an unskilful priest more than counterbalances the time occupied in these additional prayers. It is perfectly possible, without any undue haste, to say the entire Mass as it is here set down in little more than half an hour; and there are few priests who will think that too long a time for such an action."

We make no comment upon what must be the writer's idea of "undue haste"; we leave our readers to judge whether it is possible to read reverently the English Communion Office, *plus* many of the prayers of the Roman Missal, "in little more than half an hour." This book is not merely the work of a single man, for we read in the Preface "that the proof-sheets have been revised by several priests of the writer's acquaintance."

THE EXTENT OF THE RITUALISTIC MOVEMENT.

TO those Bishops and others who affect to believe that the lawlessness of the Ritualistic movement is confined to a small area we commend a careful study of the new issue of the *Tourist's Church Guide*, published by the E.C.U. They will find that, so far from the evil being limited in extent, it affects practically the whole country. We have extracted a few statistics from this useful little volume, which will show that, so far from it being checked, it is gaining ground at an alarming pace. Another piece of evidence pointing in the same direction is the official statement just issued by the E.C.U. There has been of late, we are told, a remarkable addition to the numbers of the E.C.U. From the end of July to the beginning of December 1913 persons joined the Union, and 1537 of these joined since the meeting at Bradford on September 26th, at which Lord Halifax, in his address on "The Position of the E.C.U. in face of the Present Attack," unfurled the flag of "No Surrender." His words are worth recalling :—"We refuse," he said, "to see the worship of the Church of England so degraded, and ourselves and our children deprived of what we know from long experience to be for our soul's health. We believe the Holy Eucharist, whether it be more commonly called 'the Divine Liturgy,' as in the East, or 'the Mass,' as in the West, or 'the Holy Communion,' as amongst ourselves, to be one and the same service; and we shall oppose by every means in our power any attempt to deprive us of the use of all such ceremonies, laudable customs and practices, not expressly forbidden by the Book of Common Prayer, with which the Church in the West has been used to accompany the celebration of the Holy Eucharist."

And now what of the *Tourist's Church Guide?* The book is published in alternate years, and on reference to the statistical abstract which is given as an introduction we find that since 1896 an enormous increase has taken place in the number of churches where advanced ritual is practised. *Daily Eucharist* was then celebrated in 474 churches, now it is celebrated in 613; *Eucharistic Vestments* were worn in 1632 churches, now they are worn in 2026; *Incense* was used in 307 churches, now it is used in 381; *Altar Lights* were used in 3568 churches, now they are used in 4334; *Mixed Chalice* was used in 2111 churches, now it is used in 4030; the *Eastward Position* was taken in 5964 churches, now it is taken in 7044. But these figures do not at all cover the extent of the mischief. In churches where the Eucharistic vestments are worn it may be taken for granted that what is in reality the Mass is celebrated with its accompanying illegalities, and that the doctrine involved therein is openly taught. In churches where incense is used it may also be taken for granted that both doctrine and ritual are of a very advanced character. In most of them confession is openly taught and practised, the Sacrament is often reserved, and the worship of saints is often inculcated. It may be added that the introduction of incense dates practically from the year 1882, when only nine churches used it.

The *Record* has exposed the nature of the services at many churches in London; and we have only to examine the *Guide* to see that services similar to those described are held in most of the large towns of England and Wales, as well as in a great many country villages. We give the figures relating to twenty-five well-known towns taken haphazard from the *Guide*:—

Town.	Number of Churches.		
	Incense.	Vestments.	Lights.
Birmingham	4	13	24
Brighton	6	8	16
Bristol	4	14	28
Cardiff	6	10	10
Derby	1	5	8
Exeter	2	3	12
Folkestone	1	2	5
Hastings	2	2	4
Hull	1	3	7
Ipswich	1	2	3
Leeds	2	7	22
Lincoln	1	5	11
Liverpool	5	10	16
Manchester	1	8	16
Middlesbrough	2	3	4
Newcastle	3	8	14
Northampton	1	2	4
Norwich	2	7	12
Nottingham	4	6	10
Oxford	3	14	28
Plymouth and Devonport	6	7	8
Portsmouth	2	4	9
Southampton	2	3	10
Stockport	1	4	5
Winchester	1	2	5

In the face of the facts disclosed by this table it is worse than folly to ignore the widespread character of the movement to de-Protestantise the Church of England.

NOTES.

THE summary given on page 135, of the progress of the Ritualistic movement in the country generally, renders it unnecessary to give a tabulated analysis of the services which have been described; but it may be as well to draw attention to some of the points which these reports raise.

1. It will have been noticed that in some cases the Collect, Epistle, and Gospel appointed in the Prayer Book were ignored and others substituted for them. This is not only a violation of the order of the Prayer Book, but it is one which neither a Bishop nor an Archbishop has any power to sanction, for the Act of Uniformity Amendment Act expressly excluded the Communion Office from the sphere of its operations; so that any variation from that Office, of which the Collect, Epistle, and Gospel for the day of course form a part, is a distinct breach of the law. A favourite change in this respect is to substitute a Collect from the Burial Service when celebrating what are called "Requiem Masses."

2. With regard to "non-communicating attendance," it is important to observe that there is a vast difference between permitting non-communicants to remain during the service if they wish to do so, and arbitrarily preventing those who desire to partake from approaching the Holy Table. Yet this is the effect of the regulation made in some churches, that "at the Midday Mass none will be allowed to communicate without notice being given *and permission obtained from the Vicar.*" And even in churches where no such notice is posted up it is occasionally made known that no one will be allowed to partake at the Midday Service. The rapidly growing practice of non-communicating attendance, which is being fostered by what are called "Children's Eucharists," is opposed to the whole tenour and structure of the Prayer Book, and shows a complete and even profane disregard of our Lord's

words, "Take, eat," "Drink ye all of this," when instituting the Holy Communion.

3. It is noteworthy, with regard to the use of incense, which figures so frequently in the foregoing pages, that it was not sanctioned in any form in the First Prayer Book of Edward VI., which is the "authority of Parliament" referred to in the Ornaments Rubric. Therefore, even supposing that the Rubric was ever intended to revive the ceremonial or "Ornaments" of that book, incense would still be unlawful. Moreover, every one of the counsel employed in 1866 by the English Church Union pronounced against its use, and that, too, upon their own *ex parte* case. The continued use of incense by the Romanising party in the Church of England is a striking commentary upon their professed regard for law and order. A very convenient summary of the evidence with regard to incense will be found in a pamphlet by Mr. J. T. Tomlinson, published by the Church Association.

4. Reservation of the Sacrament is urged on the ground of convenience when celebrating the Holy Communion for sick persons, notwithstanding the fact that the Church has specially provided for such cases in the Service for the Communion of the Sick. The plea of convenience is contradicted by the testimony of hundreds of clergy who have constantly to administer the Holy Communion in sick rooms, and who do not find the service too long. To anyone who has seen the genuflections and acts of adoration before the side "altars" where the Sacrament is reserved, the plea of convenience must appear to be merely an excuse. There is another aspect of the practice, which was pointed out by the Bishop of Chichester in an address to his Diocesan Conference, on November 2nd, 1898 (see *Record*, November 4th, 1898, p. 1083), viz., that as the wafer only, and not the wine, is reserved, the sick person who is thus communicated receives only a mutilated Sacrament, analogous to that offered by the Church of Rome, which denies the cup to the laity.

In fact, in all the ceremonial which has been described in the foregoing pages it will be seen that the purpose of those who practise it is to revive what is expressed in the title of this book, "The Roman Mass in the English Church."

WYCLIFFE HOUSE
(*Established* 1894),
FOR THE DIFFUSION OF
Protestant & Evangelical Literature.

Authors are respectfully invited to make use of its important publishing facilities.

PLYMOUTH
WILLIAM BRENDON AND SON
PRINTERS

CHAS. J. THYNNE'S
Books for the Present Crisis.

"A STARTLING EXPOSURE:"
The Secret History of the Oxford Movement.
By WALTER WALSH.

42nd Thousand. With new Preface, 8vo, cloth gilt. Price 3s. 6d. net.

By the same Author—"The Secret Work of the Ritualists," 2d.
"How Rome Treats the Bible," 2d.

Lawlessness in the National Church.
Letters contributed to *The Times*, July 16th, 1898, to Feb. 4th, 1899, by the Rt. Hon. Sir W. V. HARCOURT, M.P. 8vo. Paper cover, 1s. net. Cloth, 1s. 6d. net.

The Prayer Book, Articles, and Homilies.
SOME FORGOTTEN FACTS IN THEIR HISTORY WHICH MAY DECIDE THEIR INTERPRETATION.

By J. T. TOMLINSON. Illustrated. Cloth gilt, 5s. net.

Evening Communion.
The Argument for the practice stated. By the Rev. JOSHUA HUGHES-GAMES, D.C.L. (late Archdeacon of Man). Cloth gilt, 1s. 6d. net.

English Church Teaching
On Faith, Life, and Order. By the Revs. Canon GIRDLESTONE, H. C. G. MOULE, and T. W. DRURY. Third Edition. Cloth gilt, 1s. net.

By the Right Rev. BISHOP RYLE, D.D.

Light from Old Times; or, Protestant Facts and Men.

With an Introduction for Our Own Days. Large post 8vo.
Cloth gilt, 3s. 6d. net.   Morocco, gilt leaves, 10s. net.

CONTENTS:

Introduction for Our Own Days.
John Wycliffe.
Why were our Reformers burned?
John Rogers, Martyr.
John Hooper, Bishop and Martyr.
Rowland Taylor, Martyr.
Hugh Latimer, Bishop and Martyr.

John Bradford, Martyr.
Nicholas Ridley, Bishop and Martyr.
Samuel Ward.
Archbishop Laud.
Richard Baxter.
William Gurnall.
James II. and the Seven Bishops.

Bishops and Clergy of other Days;

Or, the Lives of Two Reformers (Bishops HOOPER and LATIMER) and Three Puritans (SAMUEL WARD, RICHARD BAXTER, and WILLIAM GURNALL).

With an Introduction on the Real Merits of the Reformers and the Puritans.   Crown 8vo.   Cloth gilt, 2s. 6d. net.

Principles for Churchmen.

A manual of Positive Statements on Doubtful and Disputed Points. Large Post 8vo. Cloth gilt, 3s. 6d. net.

Knots Untied.

Plain Statements on Disputed Points in Religion. Large Post 8vo.
Cloth gilt, 2s. 6d. net.

Handy Volume Edition of the above, unabridged, cloth gilt, 2s. net.

Cautions for the Times.
A Series of Essays on the Ritualistic and Romish Controversy. Edited by the late Archbishop Whately.   8vo.   Cloth, 2s. net.

Churchman to Churchmen, A.
A Series of Lectures on Matters of Controversy at the Present Day. By the Rev. A. E. BARNES-LAWRENCE, M.A., with Preface by the Rev. H. C. G. MOULE, D.D.   Fifth Edition.   Cloth, 1s.

BOOKS FOR THE PRESENT CRISIS.

Divine Ambassadors from Earth and Heaven.
By the Rev. L. G. BOMFORD. Paper cover, 6*d*. net. Cloth, 1*s*. net.

This Little Book strikes at the Root of the Present Crisis in the Church of England.

Exposition of the Lord's Supper, An.
New to the Nineteenth Century. By a Presbyter of the Church of England. 400 pp. Crown 8vo., cloth, 3*s*. 6*d*.

"A trenchant and cogent polemic against all sacerdotal views of the Lord's Supper."
British Quarterly Review.

Fallacy of Sacramental Confession, The.
Discourses delivered at St. Matthias, Poplar, by the Rev. CHAS. NEIL, M.A. Popular Edition, with Notes appended, paper cover, 6*d*.; cloth gilt, 1*s*.

"Clear, cogent, and scriptural."—Dean Lefroy, D.D.

Guide to Ecclesiastical Law, A.
For Churchwardens and Parishioners. With Plates illustrating the Romish Vestments. Cloth, 1*s*.

Guide to the Study of the Prayer Book, A.
By the Rev. Canon A. R. FAUSSET, D.D. Cloth gilt, 2*s*.

The Record says: " This 'Guide' will be found fruitful and true, and the more extended circulation which we hope it will have in this popular form will undoubtedly do good."

Indictment of the Bishops, An.
Showing how the Church of England is being corrupted and betrayed by some of them. Cloth, 1*s*. 6*d*.

Lessons from the Ordinal.
The Ordained Minister as a Preacher; as Pastor; His Inner Life before God; his Outer Life before Man. Papers read at the Islington Clerical Meeting, 1898. Cloth, 6*d*.

Ritualism and Romanism Contrary to Revelation.
By the Rev. W. MCCAW. Cloth, 1*s*. net.

Thirty-Nine Articles of the Church of England, The.
By the Rev. J. F. T. CRAMPTON, A.B., Rector of Aughrim. With Scripture Proofs and Questions with Answers. Second Edition, enlarged, cloth, '1*s*.

SMALL BOOKS

AND

PAMPHLETS ON RITUALISM.

Apostolical Succession Considered (and Refuted). By the late Archbishop Whately. Price 9*d.*

The Ritualistic Crisis. A popular explanation of Ritualism. By the Rev. H. Lindsay Young. Price 8*d.*

SIXPENCE EACH.

Auricular Confession, tested by Holy Scripture, the Formularies of the Church of England, and the Voice of Christian Antiquity. By the Rev. Gilbert Karney.

Letter on Ritualism, A, as read by the Injunctions of the Bishops in the reign of Queen Elizabeth. By the Rev. W. H. E. M'Knight.

Of the Names Protestant and Catholic, and the Principles involved in them. By the Rev. N. S. Godfrey, F.R.A.S.

Tractarian Sisters and their teaching.

The Crisis in the Church. By the Rt. Hon. Sir Wm. V. Harcourt, M.P. Being Letters to the *Times*. Authorised reprint.

FOURPENCE EACH.

Objective Presence, The. By the Rev. E. Biley, M.A.

Extreme Ritualism. By the Rev. Canon Garbett.

THREEPENCE EACH.

Apostolic Absolution. By the Rev. W. C. Moore, M.A.

Frequent Celebrations and Frequent Communions. By the Rev. M. Hobart Seymour.

Words of Institution. Are they to be understood literally or figuratively?

The Bread of Life. Thoughts on the Sacrament of the Lord's Supper.

The Breadth, Freedom, and yet Exclusiveness of the Gospel. By the late Canon Hoare.

The Meaning of the Word Church. By Archdeacon Kaye.

The Ritualistic Conspiracy. By Lady Wimborne.

TWOPENCE EACH.

A Protest against Ritualism and its Unscriptural Teachings.
By the Rev. Henry Bourn.

The Constant Presence. By the Rev. W. J. Bolton.

God's Confessional or Man's? By the Rev. G. Everard.

Sacerdotalism. By Dean Farrar.

Undoing the Work of the Reformation. By Dean Farrar.

The Bible and the Ministry. By Dean Farrar.

Evening Communion — A Divine Institution. By the Rev. J. J. Beddow.

What is Written about the Lord's Supper. By Bishop Ryle.

Questions and Answers about the Lord's Supper. By Bishop Ryle.

Anti-Ritualism. A Catechism on the Communion Office. By the Rev. W. Preston, D.D.

The True Minister. By the Ven. Archdeacon Sinclair.

What England owes to the Reformation. By Edward Hull, M.A., LL.D.

Evening Communion: Scriptural, Lawful, and Expedient. By the late Archdeacon Bardsley, D.D.

The First Step on Romanism. By the Rev. J. P. Fitzgerald.

A Pastor's Warning Words against Ritualistic Innovations. By the Rev. S. C. Baker.

Lawlessness in the Church of England. By Samuel Smith, Esq., M.P. Second Edition. 120th Thousand.

The Mass and the Confessional in the Church of England. Being the popular Report of the Albert Hall Meeting, January 31, 1899.

CHAS. J. THYNNE'S

RITUALISM IN THE CHURCH OF ENGLAND.

UNDER this title CHAS. J. THYNNE is now publishing a Series of Pamphlets for the People, written both by Churchmen and Nonconformists.

These pamphlets will plainly demonstrate the inalienable right of the people of this land to worship God in their churches according to the spiritual principles of the Reformation and the Standards of Doctrine of the National Church, and will expose the doctrines and practices of those who are trying to **UNDO THE WORK OF THE REFORMATION**. The price of each pamphlet is 2*d.*, or 14*s.* per 100.

SPECIAL TERMS FOR DISTRIBUTION.

No. 1. **The Rights and Duties of Lay Churchmen.** By the Right Rev. Bishop Ryle, D.D.

No. 2. **Speeches of Samuel Smith, Esq., M.P., and of the Right Hon. Sir William Harcourt, M.P.**, in the House of Commons, June 16th and 21st, 1898, on Illegal Services in the Church of England and Romish Teaching. 60th Thousand.

No. 3. **The Teaching of the Church of England Concerning the Lord's Supper, or Holy Communion.**

No. 4. **What Ritualists teach the Young.** An Address by Samuel Smith, Esq., M.P., on Ritualism and Elementary Education, with an Appendix of Extracts from Ritualistic Books for Children.

No. 5. **The Bible: the True Charter of British Liberties.** By the late Canon Hugh Stowell.

No. 6. **What Ritualists teach and What the Church of England Teaches concerning Absolution and Confession.** By the Rev. W. Preston, D.D.

OTHERS TO FOLLOW.

PAMPHLETS FOR THE PRESENT CRISIS.

PRICE ONE PENNY EACH, OR SEVEN SHILLINGS PER HUNDRED.

The Atonement: a Witness against Sacerdotalism. By the Rev. H. C. G. Moule, D.D.

The Position and Rights of the Laity. By the Rev. Canon Jenkins, M.A.

Shall I Fast? By the Rev. W. B. R. Caley, M.A.

Shall I Confess? By the Rev. W. B. R. Caley, M.A.

The Teaching of the Catacombs. By the Ven. Archdeacon Sinclair.

Is Ritualism in the Church of England Popular?

The Position of Protestant Churchmen in the Present Crisis. By the Rev. J. B. Mylius.

Shepherd or no Shepherd? A Plea for the Christian Ministry. By a Layman.

To Whom shall we Confess, and Why? By the Rev. C. H. Gibson, B.A.

Benefits of the Reformation. By Archdeacon Sinclair.

The Due Limits of Ritual in the Church of England. By the Right Rev. Lord Bishop of Sodor and Man.

The Papacy as Prefigured by Daniel. By the Rev. W. B. Sandford.

Some of the Main Causes of Alienation from the Church. By the Rev. H. C. Wisdom.

PAMPHLETS FOR THE PRESENT CRISIS.

By BISHOP RYLE.

ONE PENNY EACH, OR SEVEN SHILLINGS PER HUNDRED.

His Presence: Where is it?
Let us Hold Fast our Profession.
Perilous Times.
Are you Fighting?
Prove, and Hold Fast.
The Position of the Laity.
What is Evangelical Religion?
Buy a Sword.
What do we owe to the Reformation?
Are there few? A Question for the Times.
Is it Peace? A Kind Enquiry.
The City! or, The Sight which Stirred St. Paul.
Which Class? A Question for Everybody.
Are you Weary? A Kind Enquiry.
Looking unto Jesus. Heb. xii. 2.
Prove all Things. A Tract on Private Judgment.
The Present Distress. An Address for 1898–99. Popular Edition.

PRICE SIXPENCE PER DOZEN.

What is Ritualism, and why ought it to be opposed: Where does this Road lead to?—A Question about Ritualism.

COMPLETE CATALOGUES POST-FREE.

London:
CHAS. J. THYNNE,
Wycliffe House,
6, Great Queen Street, Lincoln's Inn, W.C.

www.ingramcontent.com/pod-product-compliance
Lightning Source LLC
Chambersburg PA
CBHW030318170426
43202CB00009B/1052